SECESSION AND STATE CREATION

WHAT EVERYONE NEEDS TO KNOW®

JAMES KER-LINDSAY AND MIKULAS FABRY

OXFORD
UNIVERSITY PRESS

OXFORD
UNIVERSITY PRESS

Oxford University Press is a department of the University of Oxford.
It furthers the University's objective of excellence in research, scholarship,
and education by publishing worldwide.

Oxford is a registered trade mark of Oxford University
Press in the UK and certain other countries.

"What Everyone Needs to Know" is a registered trademark of
Oxford University Press.

Published in the United States of America by Oxford University Press
198 Madison Avenue, New York, NY 10016, United States of America.

© Oxford University Press 2023

Library of Congress Cataloging-in-Publication Data
Names: Ker-Lindsay, James, 1972– author. | Fabry, Mikulas, author.
Title: Secession and state creation : what everyone needs to know /
James Ker-Lindsay and Mikulas Fabry.
Description: New York, NY : Oxford University Press, 2022. |
Series: What everyone needs to know |
Includes bibliographical references and index.
Identifiers: LCCN 2022021554 (print) | LCCN 2022021555 (ebook) |
ISBN 9780190494056 (hardback) | ISBN 9780190494049 (paperback) |
ISBN 9780190494070 (epub)
Subjects: LCSH: Secession. | Newly independent states. |
Recognition (International law)
Classification: LCC JC327 .K47 2022 (print) | LCC JC327 (ebook) |
DDC 320.1/5—dc23/eng/20220729
LC record available at https://lccn.loc.gov/2022021554
LC ebook record available at https://lccn.loc.gov/2022021555

DOI: 10.1093/wentk/9780190494056.001.0001

1 3 5 7 9 8 6 4 2

Paperback printed by Sheridan Books, Inc., United States of America
Hardback printed by Bridgeport National Bindery, Inc., United States of America

CONTENTS

2 Old Rules: Secession and State Creation, 1776–1945   **40**

5 Independence and the Institutions of Statehood   110

6 Joining the International Community   137

7 Current Questions and Future Directions   157

ABBREVIATIONS

AU	African Union
ASEAN	Association of Southeast Asian States
CARICOM	Caribbean Community
CIS	Commonwealth of Independent States
EBRD	European Bank for Reconstruction and Development
EBU	European Broadcasting Union
ECOWAS	Economic Community of West African States
EPLF	Eritrean People's Liberation Front
ETA	Basque Homeland and Liberty
EU	European Union
FRY	Federal Republic of Yugoslavia
FAO	Food and Agriculture Organization
FIFA	the governing body for world soccer
FRETILIN	Revolutionary Front for an Independent East Timor
FRG,	Federal Republic of Germany (West Germany)
FYROM	Former Yugoslav Republic of Macedonia
GAM	Free Aceh Movement
GCC	Gulf Cooperation Council
ICJ	International Court of Justice
GDR,	German Democratic Republic (East Germany)

IAEA	International Atomic Energy Agency
ICAO	International Civil Aviation Organization
IFIs	international financial institutions
IMF	International Monetary Fund
IMO	International Maritime Organization
INTERPOL	International Criminal Police Organization
IOC	International Olympic Committee
IOM	International Organization for Migration
IRA	Irish Republican Army
ISO	International Organization for Standardization
ITU	International Telecommunications Union
KRG	Kurdistan Regional Government
LTTE	Liberation Tigers of Tamil Eelam
NATO	North Atlantic Treaty Organization
NKR	Nagorno-Karabakh Republic
NORAD	North American Aerospace Defense Command
NSGT	Non-Self-Governing Territory
OAS	Organization of American States
OIC	Organization of Islamic Cooperation
ONUC	Opération des Nations Unies au Congo
OSCE	Organization for Security and Cooperation in Europe
PKK	Kurdistan Workers' Party
PMR	Pridnestrovian Moldavian Republic
PRC	People's Republic of China
ROC	Republic of China
R2P	Responsibility to Protect
RS	Republika Srpska
RSK	Republic of Serbian Krajina
RSS	Regional Security System
SADR	Sahrawi Arab Democratic Republic
SFRY	Socialist Federal Republic of Yugoslavia
SNP	Scottish National Party
SPLA	Sudan People's Liberation Army

TRNC	Turkish Republic of Northern Cyprus
UAE	United Arab Emirates
UAR	United Arab Republic
UDI	Unilateral declaration of independence
UEFA	Union of European Football Associations
UK	United Kingdom of Great Britain and Northern Ireland
UN	United Nations
UNESCO	UN Educational, Scientific, and Cultural Organization
UPU	Universal Postal Union
US	United States of America
USSR	Union of Soviet Socialist Republics
WHO	World Health Organization
WTO	World Trade Organization
ZANU	Zimbabwe African National Union
ZAPU	Zimbabwe African People's Union

INTRODUCTION ("ARE ALL STATES EQUAL?")

We live in a world of sovereign states. They are the fundamental building blocks of the international system. And yet this system is in a period of unprecedented flux.

Around the world, scores of separatist groups and territories are pursuing independence, either peacefully or through armed force. Not since the heyday of decolonization in the late 1950s and 1960s have the topics of secession and state-creation attracted so much international attention. From Kosovo's declaration of independence in 2008, the same year as Russia's decision to recognize Abkhazia and South Ossetia, through to Scotland's independence referendum in 2014, the attempts by Catalonia and Kurdistan to break away from Spain and Iraq in 2017, and the prolonged war between Russia and Ukraine over Crimea and the secessionist regions of Donetsk and Luhansk, which entered a violent new phase in early 2022, separatism has rarely been more newsworthy. Some see Brexit—the United Kingdom's (UK) departure from the European Union (EU)—as a form of secessionism. Then there are the little-known campaigns, or the potentially emerging ones, such as Ambazonia in the Central African nation of Cameroon or Tigray in Ethiopia. While most have little chance of success, others are tomorrow's states in-the-making. Somaliland, Bougainville, Chuuk, and Greenland, all territories, could well be future members of the United Nations (UN).

Meanwhile, the nature of statehood itself is being called into question and in a variety of ways. The idea that all sovereign states are truly equal is an illusion. The assumption that the United States, China, and India are the same as the tiny Pacific island states is a legal fiction. While we say that states are the heart of the international system, many other entities now enjoy extraordinary power and influence in the international system, including the EU, the UN, and even major global corporations. Which wields more international clout: Google or Grenada? Then there are failed states, countries that are formally recognized and part of the UN but wholly incapable of meeting the demands and responsibilities of statehood. These territories have become hotbeds for organized crime, piracy, and terrorism, and yet we continue to treat them as sovereign states. Why?

The power of self-determination

For the past two and a half centuries, the belief in the inalienable right of peoples to decide their own future has been a driving force in international politics. The United States, the countries of Latin America, and many European states owe their existence to the power of this idea. However, the term "self-determination" only entered the vocabulary of international affairs in the early twentieth century, finding its greatest champion in US President Woodrow Wilson in the aftermath of the First World War. Now vilified for his abhorrent views on race and segregation in the United States, Wilson in his day stood at the forefront of efforts to give national communities their own states. Even today, the so-called "Wilsonian Vision" of national homelands remains the most powerful articulation of the rights of peoples to decide their own political and national destinies.

However, it was at the end of the Second World War that the world really saw the notion of self-determination come into its own as the European powers began withdrawing from their colonial empires in Africa and Asia. Explicitly outlined in the very first article of the Charter of the United Nations, the general acceptance of the right of self-determination led to a proliferation of new countries in the decades that followed. When the UN was founded, in 1945, it had just 51 members. Today membership stands at 193.

The principle of self-determination is deceptively alluring. While the idea of statehood remains an aspiration for many peoples around the world, history has shown that achieving independence from another national entity—usually known in the parlance of international law as the "parent state"— is fiendishly difficult. Few are willing to part with territory. Whether due to cultural or historical attachment to the land in question, the economic costs of losing a province, or just plain national pride, the parent states meet any attempt by a region or minority to secede with fierce opposition. Indeed, these states are often prepared to use force to prevent a territory from breaking away. A string of bitter and bloody secessionist wars in Africa, South Asia, the Caucasus, and the Balkans over the past fifty years are testament to just how far parent states are willing to go to preserve their territorial integrity in the face of a separatist threat.

Even if a territory manages to persuade the parent state from which it wants to secede to let it go its own way, the process of negotiating a separation can be arduous. A vast array of issues need to be tackled. These can range from the division of assets through to key decisions over its membership of international bodies. For example, it took a decade after Yugoslavia collapsed in the early 1990s for the five former republics to conclude an Agreement on Succession covering such issues as diplomatic properties, state archives, and pension payments.

As well as stiff opposition from their parent states, territories vying for independence often face strong resistance from other states. The harsh reality is that an aspiring country rarely finds support from the wider international community. Members of that community are often extremely cautious about secession in general and positively loathe cases where the decision to break away has taken place without the permission of the parent state. They usually punish unilateral secession by isolation and ostracization. This is hardly surprising. Only a dozen or so countries in the world are homogenous. The vast majority are made up of two or more ethnic or national communities. The fear of separatist contagion is strong. What happens to one country today could happen to their own tomorrow.

Any territory vying for independence needs to prove that it deserves to be accepted as an independent and sovereign state. The usually invoked benchmarks for acceptance are the so-called Montevideo criteria. Named after a treaty signed in 1933 in the city of Montevideo, Uruguay, and signed by countries in the Americas, the criteria require a prospective state to show that it has a defined territory, a permanent population, a truly independent government in effective control of its territory and population, and the ability to enter relations with other states. While these criteria are still invoked as the bar for international acceptance, in the decades that followed the treaty other factors started to gain prominence. For instance, a greater emphasis is now put on such issues as human rights norms and democratic values.

Even if a territory proves that it meets the conditions of statehood, the next challenge is to be formally admitted into the select club of recognized countries. This happens in two ways. First of all, there is recognition by other countries. Although legal theorists have long argued that recognition is not necessary, it provides a gateway into the international community. It is the way that states signal they accept the legitimacy of a territory as an equal—at least in formal terms. Recognition is the precursor to the establishment of formal diplomatic relations, which allows for independent states to communicate directly with one another and enter into bilateral agreements.

Second, a new state needs to become part of the international system. The ultimate seal of acceptance is membership to the UN. The initial step is to secure a recommendation from the fifteen members of the UN Security Council, including the five veto-wielding permanent members (the ultimate in statehood). This is followed by a vote in the General Assembly, which is made up of all the members of the UN.

Apart from formal UN membership, membership of other bodies can signal membership of the international community. These include various UN organizations and agencies, such as the World Bank, the International Monetary Fund (IMF), the World Health Organization (WHO), and the International Atomic Energy Agency (IAEA), to name just a few. There is also a plethora of regional entities, such as the EU, African Union (AU), North Atlantic Treaty Organization (NATO), and the Organization of Islamic Cooperation (OIC).

Then there are the seemingly mundane but nevertheless important ways that new states join the networks that link the international community of recognized states, for example by gaining a telephone dialing code or an internet domain address. Acceptance can also be signaled by membership in international sporting bodies, such as the International Olympic Committee (IOC).

An emerging new principle of secession and statehood?

While the barriers to entry into the international community remain formidable for a wannabe state, there is a growing sense that they are starting to break down. The rules concerning secession that have underpinned international order since the end of the Second World War are increasingly being challenged.

The emergence of so-called de facto states is a testament to this. At one time, the legal consensus was that a territory either was a state or it wasn't. If a territory claiming statehood met the prevailing criteria for statehood, it should be regarded as such. Now territories are emerging that have the characteristics of states—self-governing, distinct identity—but are not universally recognized as such. Kosovo and Palestine are both recognized as states by over one hundred countries in the international community. Others—such as Abkhazia, Northern Cyprus, Somaliland, and Transnistria—have received little or no recognition. In the years ahead, the international community is likely to face the emergence of more of these de facto states. This has prompted many to ask if the time has come to reconsider the way in which the international community admits new members into its ranks.

Regardless of how the debates over the terms of independence and statehood evolve in the future, we can be sure of one thing. Given how much rides on it—millions of lives, the fates of nations—the question of secession and the emergence of new states will remain a key challenge to international peace and security in the years ahead.

1

STATEHOOD AND SECESSION IN INTERNATIONAL POLITICS

What is a state?

While the concept of statehood has existed for hundreds of years, it is perhaps surprising to learn that the formally accepted definition of a "state" only emerged in 1933. The Montevideo Convention on the Rights and Duties of States is generally understood to provide the clearest and most succinct legal description of statehood. According to the convention, a state has to have four key attributes: (1) a defined territory, (2) a permanent population, (3) a government, and (4) a capacity to enter relations with other states.

In a broader sense, a state is best understood as the fundamental political and legal unit of the contemporary international system. While other actors may exist in international politics, such as international organizations and multinational corporations, the system itself is built around sovereign states as distinct and independent political units.

What is sovereignty?

At the heart of statehood lies the principle of constitutional independence, better known as "sovereignty." Internally, this gives a state supreme legal authority over its territory and population. Formally at least, a state has the last word over matters of governance within its borders. Meanwhile, externally, sovereignty means that states are considered to be independent political entities. Legally speaking, and by definition, no state is subject to another. All states are juridically equal. That said, they are bound by a package of rights and duties under international law. These include a state's duty not to interfere in another's domestic affairs and the right to expect that other states will respect its sovereignty, its independence, and its borders.

Of course, in reality, the situation is rather different. While sovereignty means that all states are technically equal in the international system and under international law, there is obviously a huge disparity between states. The world's most economically and politically powerful states and its weakest are far from equal in real terms. Nevertheless, from a formal legal perspective, the United States and the smallest Pacific island state are equal within the international system. This equality is perhaps best seen in the UN, where every member state has a single seat and just one vote in the General Assembly, its main policymaking organ.

What is a "defined territory"?

Under international law, a state cannot exist without any territory. "Defined territory" is one of the four main attributes of statehood and there is no such thing as a country without land. However, what this means in real terms is open to debate. The minimum size of territory needed for statehood has never been established. And the actual geographic size of states varies dramatically. While the world's smallest state is the Vatican City State, which is just 44 hectares (0.17 square miles), the smallest UN member is Monaco, at just over 200 hectares (or 0.78 square miles). At the other end of the scale, the largest is the Russian Federation, which, at 17.1 million square kilometers (6.6 million square miles), is almost twice the size of the next largest state, Canada.

The term defined territory also presents other problems. For a start, defined territory does not mean fixed and universally agreed borders. Many countries come into existence with their boundaries still to be defined. For example, the final borders of both India and Israel have yet to be definitively settled, even though they declared independence in 1947 and 1948 respectively. Sometimes, border disputes and issues can arise long after independence. This could be due to a government decision to revive a dormant territorial claim, as happened when Iraq illegally invaded and annexed Kuwait in 1990 arguing that the country had once been part of Ottoman Iraq. Alternatively, border disputes can be caused by natural geographical changes, such as when a river changes course. This has led to boundary changes between the United States and Mexico, Belgium and the Netherlands, and Slovakia and Hungary.

Moreover, having a defined territory does not mean that a country's entire territory must be joined or otherwise contiguous. Leaving aside countries that are made up of groups of islands—such as the Maldives, Seychelles, Micronesia, and Cape Verde, to name just a few—there are also many states that are separated from parts of their territory by another country. In formal terms, these external pockets of land are known as "exclaves" and "enclaves."

An exclave is a piece of territory that is separated from the main territory of the state but enjoys borders with two other states or a coastal boundary. One of the most obvious examples is Alaska, which is an exclave of the United States separated from it by Canada. Kaliningrad is an exclave of the Russian Federation sandwiched between Poland and Lithuania. Nakhichevan is an exclave of Azerbaijan separated from the main part of the country by Armenia, but which also has a land border with Turkey.

Then there are enclaves. These are almost the same as exclaves. The key difference is that these pieces of a country's territory are wholly surrounded by another state. One example is Llivia, a small Spanish village that lies a couple of miles within France. The break-up of the Soviet Union also saw the emergence of many new enclaves, including the Tajik enclaves in Kazakhstan and Uzbekistan, and Uzbek enclaves in Kazakhstan. But perhaps the world's strangest enclave was Dahala Khagrabari. When it existed, it was the world's only example of a "third-order enclave": an Indian enclave within a Bangladeshi enclave within an Indian enclave within Bangladesh.[1] It dissolved in 2015, when India and Bangladesh exchanged over 160 pieces of territory in a (clearly much needed) effort to simplify their border.

Finally, enclaves should not be confused with what are known as "enclave states." These are countries whose entire territory is surrounded by another state. The three current enclave states are Lesotho, which is surrounded by South Africa, and San Marino and the Vatican City State, which are both surrounded by Italy.

Does a territory need a minimum population to be a state?

As with territory, there is no formal minimum population size. Indeed, the demographic variations between countries are just as dramatic as the geographic ones. At present, around 15 of the 193 UN members have more than 100 million inhabitants and a similar number have fewer than 100,000. The world's largest country, the People's Republic of China, has nearly 1.4 billion people. Among UN members, the smallest state is Nauru with a population of around 11,000. In real terms, there are questions about whether formal statehood would be feasible lower than this. For example, the Pacific island territory of Tokelau, which is currently under New Zealand's control, is considering a referendum on independence, even though it

---

1. "Say goodbye to the weirdest border dispute in the world," *The Washington Post*, August 1, 2015.

has a population of fewer than 1,500 residents. (Officially, and again, the smallest state is the Vatican City State. It has fewer than 800 inhabitants. However, this is rather a special case.)

Similarly, population density plays no part in determining statehood or viability. Mongolia, with the current lowest density of any country, has just two inhabitants per square kilometer (or a little over five people per square mile). Meanwhile, Australia, Iceland, Libya, Namibia, and Suriname all exist with around three inhabitants per square kilometer. The most densely populated states in the world are Monaco, with 25,300 people per square kilometer, and Singapore, with 8,000 per square kilometer.

What does "government" mean in the context of statehood?

The third criterion for statehood under the Montevideo Convention is government. This is perhaps the hardest element of statehood to pin down. No precise definition of "government" has ever been given. Even the Montevideo Convention was quiet on the issue. However, it is possible to get some idea of what it might mean from the way countries have behaved toward new states in the past.

Historically, it was expected that the government of any new state should be "effective." This was generally understood to mean that it had to be established by the population of the state and thus be independent of all external authorities and that it had to control the bulk of its population and territory. However, while the notion of government presupposes some form of an administrative apparatus, this was never meant to be an assessment of whether the government in place could in fact govern well. Instead, it was merely meant to signify whether the population at large was willing to accept the state as its ruler in their everyday lives. If people kept respecting domestic laws, serving in the military, paying taxes, and, above all, avoided active anti-governmental resistance—in other words, if they collectively demonstrated what was referred to as "habitual obedience" to the new rulers—then the new government's control was deemed effective. To this extent, "effective control" was perfectly compatible with ineffective administration, widespread poverty, official corruption, deficient bureaucracy, and a host of other phenomena associated with a weak state.

In the post-colonial era, effective control has been largely abandoned as a strict criterion of statehood. This is not to say that the new states that have emerged have lacked effective government. Rather, it was not considered to be a necessary condition for their recognition. Many new states created by decolonization had barely any institutions of effective government. The Congo is a good example. It had just a couple of dozen university graduates when it became independent from Belgium in 1960. More recently, South Sudan, which became independent in 2011, also had very little capacity for effective government when it achieved statehood.

Moreover, there is no requirement for "effective government" to be self-sustaining once a state is recognized. Many countries, often referred to as "failed states," have continued to be regarded as states even though they no longer have a functioning administrative system. Perhaps the best example is Somalia. Despite collapsing into a patchwork of warring fiefdoms in the early 1990s, it has remained a member of the UN.

What does the ability to enter relations with other states mean?

The fourth and final characteristic of a state according to the Montevideo Convention is an ability to enter relations with other states. Historically, this was considered to be just another element of effective government. However, within the convention it was singled out as a separate element—perhaps to try to emphasize the point that statehood was about international legal personality.

Today, many observers believe that this attribute should no longer be given the same significance as the other three criteria for statehood. We live in a world in which any number of organizations and institutions can now interact with countries on a very similar footing as sovereign states. For instance, the UN and the EU maintain missions around the world and their officials enjoy diplomatic rights and privileges. Neither are states. Likewise, there are many companies and nongovernmental organizations that have extensive contacts with governments around the world. Indeed, they may often be regarded as far more significant actors than many states. For example, most countries would pay far more attention to a senior executive of one of the world's leading technology or energy companies than a high-level member of the government of a small Pacific or Caribbean island state.

How many states are there?

This is a matter of considerable debate. If we accept membership of the UN as the best and most reliable indicator of widespread state acceptance, there are currently 193 states. In addition, there are two territories that are nominally states but are in a special relationship with New Zealand known as free association. These are Niue and the Cook Islands. Although they are not members of the UN as a whole, they have their own seats in a number of UN institutions, such as WHO. As a result, they have a rather ambiguous status in the international system. Then there are four further territories that are not members of the UN but are widely considered to be states or effectively operate as such for many international purposes: The Holy See (Vatican), Palestine, Kosovo, and Taiwan.

In addition, there are territories that claim independence, and possess the attributes of statehood, but are largely or completely unrecognized by other states. Examples in this category include Somaliland, Nagorno-Karabakh, Transnistria, Abkhazia, South Ossetia, and Northern Cyprus. The exact number of these "states"—often referred to as de facto states— is unclear as there is considerable difference between scholars and practitioners about whether particular territories meet the necessary conditions for statehood.

For these reasons, the most usually cited figure is the number of UN members plus any or all of the others named in the previous paragraphs. Broadly speaking, therefore, there are a little under 200 "independent" states around the world.

What is the difference between a state and a country?

While both words essentially have the same dictionary definition—an entity with a defined territory, a permanent population, and a government—the term state is usually used instead of country in international legal settings. However, in everyday language, the two words are often used interchangeably. (Indeed, both terms are used in this book—if only to add some variation and avoid endlessly repeating the word state.)

The problem is that this interchangeability doesn't always apply. While the terms state and country are often used to describe sovereign and independent territories, both can also be used to describe lower-level, subnational units. For instance, the UK, a state, is officially made up of three countries: England, Scotland, and Wales. (Northern Ireland is also sometimes referred to as a country but is officially classed as a province or constituent unit.) Similarly, the term state can often be used to describe a federal unit rather than an independent sovereign state. Hence, the United States of America, a country, is made up of states.

To add to the confusion, and to further complicate the answer given to the previous question, while the UN has 193 member states, the International Organization for Standardization (ISO), the global body that helps to draw up agreed standards across a wide range of fields, actually lists 249 separate country codes. This includes territories that enjoy considerable autonomy or a distinct identity within an established state—such as Greenland, which is an autonomous dependent territory of Denmark, and Hong Kong, which is a Special Administrative

Region of the People's Republic of China (PRC)—but are not actually independent.[2]

A state can therefore be part of a country, just as a country can be part of a state. Ultimately, how the terms should be understood rather depends on the context in which they are being used.

What is secession?

Secession comes from the Latin for withdrawal. It refers to the process whereby a territory and its population breaks away from an existing state and either establishes a new country or unites with another one. In practice, almost all cases of secession now lead to the creation of an independent state. There are very few instances in the post-1945 era of a territory that has successfully seceded from one country and joined another. Moreover, few current secessionist movements seem interested in uniting with another territory. One notable exception is of course Northern Ireland. Those who want to see an end to British rule over the province support unification with the Republic of Ireland. There is no talk of an independent Northern Irish state.

2. "Country Codes—ISO 3166," International Organization for Standardization https://www.iso.org/iso-3166-country-codes.html. Territories that have ISO country codes, but are not UN members, include: Aland Islands, American Samoa, Antarctica, Bouvet Island, British Indian Ocean Territory, Christmas Island, Falkland Islands, Faroe Islands, French Guiana, French Polynesia, French Southern Territories, Gibraltar, Greenland, Guernsey, Heard Island and the McDonald Islands, Hong Kong, Jersey, Macao, Montserrat, New Caledonia, Pitcairn, Reunion, Saint Barthelemy, Saint Martin, Saint Pierre and Miquelon, Sint Maarten, South Georgia and the South Sandwich Islands, Svalbard and Jan Mayen, Turks and Caicos Islands, United States Minor Outlying Islands, British Virgin Islands, Virgin Islands (US), and Western Sahara. England, Scotland, and Wales do not enjoy their own ISO country codes. Instead, they are officially listed as subdivisions of the United Kingdom.

There are two forms of secession: "consensual secession" and "unilateral secession." Consensual secession occurs when the territory breaks away with the permission of the state it is leaving—usually called the "parent state." Examples of consensual secession include Eritrea's independence from Ethiopia, in 1993, and South Sudan's split from Sudan, in 2011. Unilateral secession occurs against the will of the parent state. Historically, the large majority of cases of secession have been unilateral. Most of the cases of secession examined later in this book—such as Northern Cyprus, Kosovo, Somaliland, and Abkhazia—are examples of unilateral secession.

Why do countries tend to oppose secession?

Although some countries are willing to allow a territory to become independent, most strongly oppose an attempt by a part of their territory to break away. Indeed, even those states that do eventually allow secession will have spent many years, if not decades, trying to prevent it from happening. There are many reasons for this. For a start, a country's borders will usually have an important symbolic meaning and touch on its core identity. Children are often taught from a young age to recognize and draw a map of their country. Even as adults, people are confronted with images of their countries every day, for example on weather forecasts. Some countries, such as Cyprus and Kosovo, even have the map of the country on their national flags. For these reasons, a change of borders can fundamentally challenge a country's most basic sense of itself. Tied to this, the attachment to a territory may be based on deep-rooted historical or cultural reasons. For instance, it may contain sites of special religious significance.

While an emotional or historical attachment to a territory is certainly an important factor, there are many other reasons why states are reluctant to accept secession, even when it might be in their interests to do so (such as to ease tension and foster peace). The most obvious is money. The land in question could have important economic value. For example, it might contain valuable natural resources, such as oil or gas, as was long the case with Scotland. It might be a fertile agricultural region, a widely cited reason for US opposition to the attempted secession by the Confederate States of America. It might be an industrial heartland, such as Donbas in Ukraine, or a financial center, as is the case with Catalonia in Spain. Alternatively, it may have important strategic significance, such as providing access to the sea. This was a prominent reason why landlocked Ethiopia opposed Eritrea's efforts to secede.

Then there is the snowball or contagion effect. A parent state may fear that if one part of its territory secedes, others will follow. This was part of the reason Congo put up such strong resistance when Katanga tried to secede, in 1960. Again, this is also a very real worry for Spain. If Catalonia breaks away, will this open the way for the Basque Country to pursue independence as well?

Finally, countries are sometimes reluctant to give up a territory when secession has occurred after a civil war or external intervention. While some may see the logic of letting the land go, especially if it brings about peace, there is often a deep reluctance to legalize an act of forced secession. For many observers, this goes part of the way toward explaining why Cyprus opposes the secession of Northern Cyprus, why Georgia stands against the independence of Abkhazia, and why Azerbaijan refuses to contemplate an independent Nagorno-Karabakh.

Of course, there are very few cases where the reasons a parent state opposes secession can be reduced to just one of these factors. While one reason may well predominate, it is almost always linked to several other issues.

Why do other countries oppose secession?

Here again, we need to differentiate between consensual and unilateral secession. In cases where secession takes place with the blessing of the country it is breaking away from, the new state is usually—if not always—accepted by the international community. For example, South Sudan was quickly admitted to the UN following its independence from Sudan, in 2011. Likewise, Montenegro found little problem in gaining international acceptance when it split from Serbia in 2006 following an internationally accepted referendum.

In contrast, unilateral secession is usually met with strong and unyielding opposition from the international community. Unlike times past, when a territory would often be recognized if it proved its ability to exist as an independent state, in the post-decolonization era such territories can exist for decades without acceptance. Somaliland is an excellent case in point. Although it clearly meets the four criteria for statehood under the Montevideo Convention, and in fact was briefly a sovereign independent state following the end of British colonial rule in 1960, it has not been recognized by any country since it broke away from Somalia and reclaimed its independence in 1991.

This ingrained opposition to unilateral secession is based on the general fear among states of endorsing something that may come back to haunt them. After all, a mere handful of the 193 members of the UN are ethnically homogenous. If a country is seen to endorse a case of unilateral secession, it may embolden its own separatists to act. Alternatively, it may lay itself open to charges of hypocrisy if it then denies independence to a part of its own territory.

More generally, there is also a deep-rooted worry that if unilateral secession is accepted in one instance, it may open the way for other territories to follow suit. This could have far-reaching consequences. At worst, an unfettered right of independence would lead to an anarchic and unmanageable international order. As the former UN Secretary-General Boutros Boutros-Ghali famously noted, "if every ethnic, religious or linguistic group claimed statehood, there would be no limit to fragmentation, and peace, security and economic well-being for all would become ever more difficult to achieve."[3] Indeed, if every ethnic or linguistic group that wanted to become independent could do so, the UN would not be an organization of 200 or so members but one of five or six thousand! In other words, the general opposition to unilateral secession is about maintaining national unity and international order. In fact, as will be shown in Chapter 3, since 1945, only one country, Bangladesh, has unilaterally declared independence and managed to obtain general international recognition and membership of the UN.

What is a unilateral declaration of independence?

As the term suggests, a unilateral declaration of independence (UDI) is the formal instrument used by a territory to announce that it is now a sovereign state in cases where the secession is taking place without the permission of the parent state. As it is most usually done in the name of a people seeking independence, the declaration is typically issued by a legislative or quasi-legislative body.

Importantly, in 2010, the International Court of Justice, the UN's judicial arm, ruled that UDIs are not in fact contrary to general international law.[4] Addressing the case of Kosovo's unilateral declaration of independence from Serbia, the court stated that unless there is a specific prohibition on unilateral secession—for example, a UN resolution preventing independence or a peace treaty outlawing secession—any territory is perfectly at liberty to declare that it is a state. However, in

3. "An Agenda for Peace: Preventive Diplomacy, Peacemaking and Peace-Keeping," Report of the Secretary-General Pursuant to the Statement Adopted by the Summit Meeting of the Security Council on 31 January 1992, Security Council Document S/24111, June 17, 1992, paragraph 17.
4. International Court of Justice, "Accordance with international law of the unilateral declaration of independence in respect of Kosovo (Request for Advisory Opinion)," July 22, 2010.

truth, any such declaration will mean very little on its own. It is merely a statement. In fact, anyone could declare any bit of land to be independent. But it would not make it a state. Ultimately, what matters is whether the new state can cement its existence and whether its claim to independence is eventually accepted by the wider international community.

While the term UDI has negative connotations, in formal legal terms it merely indicates that the declaration of independence has taken place without the agreement of the two sides in question—the territory breaking away and the state that has internationally recognized sovereignty over that territory. For instance, when Kosovo declared independence, it deliberately used the term "coordinated declaration of independence" to denote that it took the decision with key international partners that supported its sovereign statehood and avoided the term unilateral. However, the fact that the decision was opposed by Serbia, the state it was formally seceding from, means that officially its declaration is classed as a UDI.

How can parent states respond to an act of unilateral secession?

As one would expect, a UDI will usually be vigorously opposed by the parent state. This can be done in a few ways. For example, it may formally annul the declaration and inform the international community that it has no legal effect. It might also take other steps to emphasize that the UDI is invalid.

A good example was Catalonia's attempt to unilaterally secede from Spain in 2017. After having used its police to disrupt the independence referendum organized by the Catalan government, Spain took strong action following the subsequent UDI in the Catalan parliament. Not only did it dissolve the Catalan government and reimpose direct rule over the Catalan autonomous region, but it also prosecuted Catalan independence leaders. This saw many of them given lengthy jail sentences. (Interestingly, the Catalan case also showed that harsh reactions to unilateral secession are not just confined to undemocratic or authoritarian states. Even liberal democracies can react very strongly when facing a unilateral secession.) Even when a UDI is suppressed by a parent state, it has rarely eradicated secessionist sentiment. Indeed, it is not unheard of for an aspiring state to repeat its declaration of independence under more favorable circumstances. A good example is the Dominican Republic, which declared independence in 1821 and 1844. A UDI therefore usually marks the beginning, not the end, of a quest for statehood.

How many secessionist movements are there in the world?

This is an incredibly difficult question to answer. There is huge variation in the size and scope of secessionist movements. Should the figure include only territories that are actively pursuing statehood through political or military means, or should it include peoples that have expressed merely a vague aspiration for independence? In either case, what would be a credible threshold of support for inclusion? Should it be a group with 1,000 members, 100, or maybe just 10? In cases of proscribed organizations, such as the Irish Republican Army (IRA), the Kurdistan Workers' Party (PKK), and Basque Homeland and Liberty (ETA), there is no way to gather accurate figures for membership or even support.

One often-cited reference is the Unrepresented Nations and Peoples Organization (UNPO). This currently has around forty-five members. While some of the members are recognizable, such as Somaliland, Catalonia, Taiwan, Abkhazia, and Aceh, others are rather less familiar, such as Sulu (The Philippines), Savoy (Italy), Oromo (Ethiopia), Western Togoland (Ghana), Kabylia (Algeria), and Barotseland (Zambia). However, even this list is problematic. Several members, such as the Afrikaners (South Africa) and Batwa (Rwanda), do not appear to seek actual independence. Instead, they are pursuing minority or cultural rights within existing states. Also, there are many movements that are not part of UNPO. In fact, many of the most major secessionist territories are not listed—such as Scotland, Flanders, and Quebec. Likewise, none of the prominent US independence movements are represented. For example, Alaska, Hawaii, Texas, and Vermont, the four US states that have long-standing, though not necessarily widely supported, secessionist movements are notably missing from the UNPO line up. And yet, Washington, DC (the District of Columbia), is a member due to its lack of federal representation within the United States.

All things considered, it is probably fair to say that there are about 30–60 notable secessionist efforts currently underway around the world that are credibly pursuing statehood, either by military or diplomatic means. The most recognizable cases would include, but certainly not be limited to, Nagorno-Karabakh (Azerbaijan); Flanders (Belgium); Republika Srpska (Bosnia and Herzegovina); Quebec (Canada); Taiwan and Tibet (China); Northern Cyprus (Cyprus); Greenland (Denmark); the Faroe Islands (Denmark); Tigray, Oromia, and Ogaden (Ethiopia); Corsica (France); Abkhazia and South Ossetia (Georgia); Western Togoland (Ghana); West Papua (Indonesia); Kurdistan (Iraq); the Tuaregs (Mali and Niger); Transnistria (Moldova); Balochistan (Pakistan); Bougainville (Papua New Guinea); Somaliland (Somalia); Catalonia and the Basque Country (Spain); Ambazonia (Cameroon); Scotland and Northern Ireland (UK); and Puerto Rico (United States).

However, as this list perhaps shows, deciding on which countries to include is more of an art than a science. While all these cases involve long-standing claims to statehood and enjoy at least some popular backing—although in many cases support for independence is far from a majority point of view—there are few, if any, specific criteria that draw them all together in any formal way. It tends to be little more than what feels objectively credible—and what perhaps subjectively feels like a notable case.

Why do territories and peoples want to secede?

Just as there are many reasons why states will try to stop a part of their territory from breaking away, so there are various reasons why a particular community may wish to secede from one country and to form their own. Most obviously, the population may want to pursue independence simply because they belong to a different ethnic or religious community from the rest of the population and wish to have their own homeland. However, on its own, this cannot explain secession. After all, there are many situations where a minority community has not expressed a wish to secede.

Usually, there will be other, and often multiple, additional factors driving the campaign for independence. For example, a group may have suffered discrimination, political oppression, or human rights abuses at the hands of the parent state or may have been systematically denied the right to control their own political or cultural affairs. Alternatively, discontent may be focused on economic factors. A territory may be wealthier than the rest of the country and feel that it is unfairly subsidizing other parts of the state. Likewise, there may be a sense that the central state is exploiting their labor or their natural resources and that they would be richer on their own. For instance, this was a powerful sentiment driving Slovenia's wish to break away from Yugoslavia and Catalonia's attempt to break away from Spain.

At other times, the wish to secede may be driven by an unresolved historical grievance, or a sense that an opportunity for independence had been denied in the past and should now be corrected. For example, this is very powerful in the case of the Kurds, who, having been promised a national homeland after the First World War, saw the proposed territory of their state divided between Turkey and Iraq. Finally, secession may be the result of a desire to leave one country and join ethnic brethren in another state. This can be seen in Northern Ireland, Crimea, and Republika Srpska.

Can states use armed force to prevent secession?

Historically, international law has accepted the right of states to use armed force against internal challenges to their constitutional order. As a result, most serious secessionist campaigns have descended into violence at some point. Even independence efforts that eventually succeeded—such as Brazil's secession from Portugal in 1825, or Finland's secession from Russia in 1917—were forcibly resisted at some point. In fact, bloodless consensual secessions have been very rare indeed. The few examples include Norway's secession from Sweden in 1905, Iceland's separation from Denmark in 1944, and Singapore's departure from Malaysia in 1965.

While the use of force was generally accepted in the past, since the end of the Cold War a debate has emerged on the issue. This was linked to the widespread atrocities that occurred during the Balkans conflicts of the 1990s. In some instances, the use of extreme violence eventually led to war crimes trials.[5] However, the cases were not about the right to use armed force, as such. Instead, they focused on the way that armed force was used. Indeed, there does not appear to have been any discernible shift among states regarding the fundamental right of states to use force against armed separatist groups. Russia, Croatia, and Sri Lanka, among others, have used armed force against secessionist movements within their borders without encountering objections from the UN or any other international organization to their fundamental right to do so—even if the way force was applied was met with widespread condemnation.

5. See the International Criminal Tribunal for the Former Yugoslavia (ICTY) http://www.icty.org.

What is "remedial secession"?

One of the most interesting and controversial debates to have emerged in discussions over secession in recent years is the concept of "remedial secession." This refers to situations where a territory declares independence as an emergency self-defense measure in the face of gross human rights violations by the parent state, such as genocide, ethnic cleansing, or crimes against humanity.

Although the idea has been championed by some since the 1970s, the concept drew renewed attention as a natural continuation of discussions that emerged at the turn of the millennium over the concept of Responsibility to Protect (R2P).[6] This idea is based on the view that states are obliged to protect their populations from atrocities on their territory. If they are unable to do so, or indeed if the state is itself committing the atrocities, then the international community has the right, if not the duty, to step in to halt these abuses—even if this is a violation of traditional rules of state sovereignty.

Remedial secession takes this a step further. Its proponents argue that territories whose population faces mass atrocities should have the right to secede, and be recognized by the international community, as a means of securing their own survival. Once the sovereignty of the former parent state is no longer accepted, the way is then open for third countries to offer the new state a range of support, including military assistance.

The principle of remedial secession is, understandably, highly contentious. So far, it has not gained much traction among political decisionmakers. In large part, this is because states are obviously very worried about legitimizing such a far-reaching doctrine. Unlike other forms of intervention, such

6. "The Responsibility to Protect," Report of the International Commission on Intervention and State Sovereignty, 2001; "2005 World Summit Outcome," United Nations General Assembly, September 15, 2005, paragraphs 138–139.

as the creation of a peacekeeping force, which are seen as temporary measures to stabilize a situation, recognizing a new state is a permanent move. It cannot simply be rescinded when things calm down. For the meantime, therefore, the principle of remedial secession remains largely an issue of theoretical debate.

What is irredentism?

Irredentism is the formal term used to describe a policy whereby a state advocates bringing people or territories that it regards as rightfully its own under (or back under) its sovereignty. In the past, irredentism was a very powerful source of secessionist conflict. In the nineteenth century, many nationalist movements were built around the idea of uniting a people within a nation-state homeland. For instance, modern Greece was built on the desire to unite all Greek communities around the Eastern Mediterranean. Likewise, the creation of Italy and Germany were also the products of irredentism.

In the post-1945 era, where there is a responsibility for states to respect the territorial integrity of other countries, very few states are openly irredentist. Although many countries continue to harbor irredentist sentiment to a greater or lesser degree, in most cases this does not spill over into action. For example, a poll taken in 2020 showed that 60 percent of Hungarians believed that parts of neighboring countries should still be under Hungarian sovereignty even though they were carved off in 1920 under the terms of the post–First World War Treaty of Trianon. However, Hungary has not shown any intention to act on this widely held belief. Prominent recent examples of irredentist conflicts have been Iraq's invasion and annexation of Kuwait, in 1990, and Russia's invasion and annexation of Crimea, in 2014; a rare, but powerful, example of openly irredentist policy in the twenty-first century.

Does a territory that loses its independence have a right to reclaim it?

First, it is important to differentiate between states that lost their independence involuntarily and those that chose to give up their statehood. In cases of involuntary loss of independence—through invasion, occupation, or annexation—the right to reclaim sovereignty is usually respected, even many decades later. A good example is the Soviet Union's forcible annexation of the three Baltic republics—Estonia, Latvia, and Lithuania—early in the Second World War. This was never recognized by many countries, including the United States and the UK. Therefore, when they broke away from the Soviet Union in 1991, their regained sovereignty was rapidly accepted by the wider international community.

While the situation concerning involuntary loss of independence is relatively clear cut, there is some confusion around states that voluntarily united with another state. What happens if they want to become independent sovereign states again? Many people believe that because an entity was independent before freely joining another state, it must naturally have the legal right to reclaim that independence at will. This is not the case. Unless explicitly recognized at the time of union, or by the government of the unified state afterward, once a state has joined in a union with another state it is understood to have lost its legal right to secede without permission. A very good example of this is Texas. It has no right to secede from the United States, despite having voluntarily united with it after a period as an independent state (1836–1845).

Of course, prior sovereign statehood may create a strong moral case for renewed independence. Many observers feel that Somaliland should be recognized as an independent state by reason of its voluntary decision to unite with Somalia just days after it became independent in 1960. Likewise, many feel that Scotland has a strong case for independence because it had been a separate kingdom prior to voluntarily uniting with

England in 1707. Another case is South Yemen, which united with North Yemen in 1990. Growing unhappiness with the arrangement has led some to call for South Yemen to reassert its separate statehood. However, in all three cases there is no requirement for a claim to statehood to be accepted by the international community simply based on previous independence.

The same prohibition on unilateral secession also applies to states that came about through the voluntary union of several smaller territories. Perhaps the two best examples are the United Arab Emirates (UAE) and Malaysia. Both federations are the products of unions of small states that came together during a period of decolonization. Since then, both have faced secessionist claims. Dubai threatened to leave the UAE in 1976, and Sharjah did the same in 1987. More recently, nationalists in Sabah and Sarawak have accused the Malaysian government of reneging on the terms of the agreements that brought them into the union in the early 1960s. In both cases, politicians have claimed that the territories have an "intrinsic" right of secession as they joined the union voluntarily. The national government disagrees. While Malaysia's constitution does not explicitly outlaw secession, it has made it a criminal offense specifically to call for Sabah and Sarawak to secede.

Even if an independent state voluntarily gave up its independent statehood, there is an expectation that it will still have to receive the permission of the parent state if it wishes to secede at a later stage.

Should there be a general right to secession?

This has been a long-standing philosophical debate. Within the liberal democratic tradition, there are two main schools of thought. On the one hand, there are those who advocate what is called the "primary right" view. They believe in the inherent right of self-determination for all communities that want it. There should be a general right to secession rooted in the will of a territorial majority. Interestingly, primary right theorists reject the idea that this would simply lead to chaos and fragmentation as the world splits into hundreds, if not thousands, of microstates. They argue that if a right to secession were implemented in constitutional or international law, states would have to be more responsive to the wishes of their constituent units. This would in fact enhance the quality of political representation across diverse populations. While some groups might want to break away, many others would still see strength in cooperation. It would lead to the emergence of truly democratic and representative multinational states.

On the other hand, and as discussed earlier, there are those who argue that secession should be allowed in emergency situations. Advocates of the so-called remedial right only position believe that the right of secession should be a last resort when the state is consistently and persistently violating the human rights of its population or is actively attacking its own inhabitants. They argue that if the permissive primary right view was institutionalized, the threat of secession could become a strategic bargaining tool by constituent units against the central government. This would potentially undermine the stability needed for liberal democracy as communities would be constantly making ever greater demands on the government, threatening to leave if not given what they want. This could raise the risk of near constant referendums on secession; or "neverendums" as some have called them. Remedial right only theorists therefore argue that the right to secession should arise only in exceptional cases where the parent state clearly violates the fundamental rights of its population.

Setting aside disagreements at a theoretical level, any attempt to institutionalize a right to secede internationally would face huge obstacles within the wider international community. If accepted as a binding principle, a right to secession would require third parties to actively assist territories seeking to break away. States would be highly unlikely to accept a blanket requirement that a secessionist claim within another country, whether the result of popular will or a result of human rights violations, automatically requires them to take steps to realize that goal. As already noted, even remedial secession in cases of ethnic cleansing and genocide has gained little support. In fact, the closest international society ever came to accepting a general right to secede was in the period between 1815 and 1960, when it was widely accepted that if a "civilized" territory was able to prove its effective existence as a state, then it qualified to be recognized as such. Again, this no longer applies. As noted, this explains why a territory such as Somaliland, despite clearly existing as an independent state for a number of decades, is still unrecognized.

For all these reasons, arguments for a right to secede extending beyond the currently accepted parameters—decolonization, occupation, or with the permission of the parent state—have gained limited traction.

Do any countries permit secession?

Very few states have ever explicitly accepted that their constituent units have the right to secede—either formally within their constitution or as a tacitly accepted principle. Historically, these few that did included the Socialist Federal Republic of Yugoslavia (SFRY), the Soviet Union, and the Union of Serbia and Montenegro. Today, the right is recognized in Ethiopia, Liechtenstein, Uzbekistan, and St. Kitts and Nevis.

In reality, however, even a nominal right of secession rarely translates into an easy or peaceful process of independence. In the SFRY and the Soviet Union, there were fundamental disagreements over which specific jurisdictions or peoples were entitled to the right of secession and the precise procedure by which the right could be exercised. As a result, even though secession was permitted, it nevertheless led to bloodshed.

If a constitutional right to secession exists, it is only likely to be peacefully realized in liberal democracies. But even most liberal democracies have been generally unwilling to grant an explicit constitutional right to secede. Spain's harsh measures to close down any discussion of Catalan independence is a good case in point. Even those countries that do accept a right of secession in theory and in practice, such as the UK and Canada, have only been willing to accept that their constituent units can secede when certain procedures are met, such as after a properly conducted referendum and a formal negotiation process to decide the terms of separation. Moreover, even if the right of secession is broadly recognized, it may not be able to be exercised at will. For example, following the 2014 referendum in Scotland, the British government insists that the matter is now closed for a "generation." (This is discussed in Chapter 5.)

Can a state expel a territory?

Strangely, the answer is not entirely clear. This is largely because it is a practically unknown occurrence. As noted, most of the time states will do everything in their power to hold on to territory—even if those territories are rebellious and require extensive policing. Since 1945, there has only been one example of a state expelling a territory. This was Malaysia's decision in the early 1960s to force Singapore out of the federation over deep-seated political, economic, religious, and racial differences. However, in that case, Singapore chose to accept the outcome. Its independence was therefore treated by the international community as a case of consensual secession.

Should a similar situation arise again, it is unclear what would happen if the expelled territory rejected the decision and fought to stay. Under such circumstances, it could well be the case that the main territory would actually have to secede from the territory being "expelled." The problem is that this could amount to a unilateral secession if the expelled territory still refused to split from the country in question. In this case, the international community could well be unwilling to accept the parent state's secession! Of course, this scenario is unlikely. But, as can be seen, the expulsion of a territory raises all sorts of interesting and potentially mind-bending legal and political questions.

What is recognition?

Most simply, recognition is the way in which states signal that they identify one another as sovereign and independent equals in the international system. In cases of secession, it plays a crucial role as a way of confirming the new state. When a state recognizes another state, it is indicating that it recognizes the latter's authority over a specific territory and that it should therefore enjoy certain rights and responsibilities under international law, such as the right to have its sovereignty and territorial integrity respected. Fundamentally, therefore, recognition is about acceptance and legitimacy.

On an important related note, technically speaking recognition refers only to the practice of states. International organizations, and other nonstate actors, do not, and cannot, recognize states—even if they often play a crucial role in the wider recognition process, either by admitting states as members or passing resolutions calling for members to recognize a new country. For instance, it is wrong to refer to a "UN recognized state," even though such a phrase often appears in the media.

The recognition of states should also be differentiated from several other, lesser-known forms of recognition, such as the recognition of governments. This refers to the ways in which states acknowledge political authorities as the legal administration of a country. While this was once widely used, most states have abandoned the explicit practice. This saves them from the complications of having to decide after each change of government—whether that be following a democratic election or, more significantly, a military coup d'état—whether it wishes to publicly acknowledge the new administration as legitimate or not. Still, it does sometimes happen. A good example was the decision of the United States and a number of European and Latin American countries to recognize Juan Guaidó as the interim president of Venezuela, rather than Nicolás Maduro, in January 2019. The issue also arose after the Taliban takeover of Afghanistan, in August 2021. In some circumstances, it may be necessary to implicitly recognize a government when there are several competing claimants. For instance, this arose when foreign states had to decide between the Gaddafi government in Tripoli and the authorities in Benghazi as the legitimate rulers of Libya, in 2011.

Other historic forms of recognition include the recognition of insurgency and the recognition of belligerency. These relate to the status, rights, and responsibilities of actors in armed conflicts, including the protection of noncombatants, the proper treatment of civilians in captured territories, and not engaging in acts of war in neutral territories. But even this can cause problems. Though it falls short of recognition as a state, it nevertheless gives a certain legal status to an actor and so can be seen as a form of intervention in a conflict. Perhaps the most famous case was the controversial decision by the UK, followed by other states, to recognize the belligerency between the United States and the Confederacy, in May 1861.

How important is recognition?

For decades, a heated debate has raged among legal scholars as to whether recognition was an integral element of statehood. There are two bodies of opinion. The "declarative school of thought" argues that a state comes into existence when it meets the legal criteria of statehood. If a territory has defined boundaries, a settled population, and an effective form of governance, then it is a state. Recognition is not inherently important. It is just the formal way other countries can enter diplomatic relations with the new state. In contrast, the "constitutive school of thought" believes that meeting the requirements for statehood is not enough. A territory is not a state internationally until it is recognized as such by other states. Recognition is the way countries join the wider international community and obtain full sovereign rights and obligations that other states must respect.

As things stand, the battle has seemingly been won by the declarative theorists. Most international lawyers take the view that statehood is not dependent on recognition. And yet, in many ways, the whole discussion is a pretty meaningless academic debate. In the real world, recognition is vital. Without it, states cannot enter formal relations with one another, whether legal, diplomatic, or economic. Recognition is also how states secure support for their eventual membership of the UN and a host of other regional and international organizations. For these reasons, battles are being fought every day between territories attempting to gain recognition and states trying their best to stop this from happening. For example, Kosovo and Serbia are locked in a constant struggle over recognition, with each loudly proclaiming victory when they secure a new recognition or persuade a country to withdraw its recognition. Likewise, countries as diverse as Cyprus, Georgia, and Somalia expend considerable diplomatic effort ensuring that territories that have broken away from them—Northern Cyprus, Abkhazia, and Somaliland—are not recognized.

What is non-recognition?

Just as recognition signals that a state accepts another state as a sovereign equal, the concept of non-recognition can be understood as a sign of rejection. In the case of non-recognition by individual states, it can in fact come in two different forms.

First of all, there's what we might think of as "passive non-recognition." This occurs when a country decides not to take a formal stance on a territory's sovereignty and independence. Essentially, it remains quiet on the issue. There may be several reasons for this. In some cases, recognition is withheld not because there is opposition to statehood, but because a country might not want to be the one to break ranks with the rest of the international community and recognize that independence.

This seems to be the case with Somaliland. While some countries may be adamantly opposed to its statehood, most seem well disposed toward it and would be willing to recognize it. However, no one wants to be the one to go first. Alternatively, a country may simply decide that it does not want to become embroiled in a political dispute. Again, Kosovo is a perfect example of this. While many countries have made formal statements refusing to recognize Kosovo, others have simply kept quiet on the issue and seem content to stay out of the dispute until such time as a resolution is found.

The second form of non-recognition might be best thought of as "active non-recognition." This occurs when a state openly announces that it refuses to recognize the territory in question as a state. Most usually, however, this form of non-recognition occurs when the grounds for independence violate international law. An obvious example of this would be a "state" that has come about because of an act of external force. If a country invades another country and then carves out a new "independent" state, that territory will not usually gain widespread acceptance.

In some instances, however, this form of non-recognition may be politically motivated. For example, it could be due to an ongoing conflict. Many Arab and Islamic states do not recognize Israel. The two Koreas do not recognize each other. Turkey does not recognize Cyprus. And Pakistan refuses to recognize Armenia because of its dispute with Azerbaijan over Nagorno-Karabakh. (This is often regarded as a rather odd decision, not least of all because Pakistan is not directly involved in the dispute and because Azerbaijan in fact recognizes Armenia.)

What is collective non-recognition?

While non-recognition may be taken by an individual country for its own reasons, sometimes countries will act jointly. This is known as "collective non-recognition." The most powerful form of collective non-recognition is a UN Security Council resolution condemning a unilateral declaration of independence and calling on states not to recognize it. There have been several such cases, including Katanga's attempted secession from Congo, in 1960, Rhodesia's unilateral declaration of independence ending British colonial rule, in 1965, and the attempt by Northern Cyprus to declare independence from the Republic of Cyprus, in 1983.

What is a de facto state?

In many cases of unilateral secession, the parent state is eventually able to reassert full control over the breakaway region. This happens either through negotiated reintegration or by retaking the territory by armed force. Occasionally, however, a breakaway territory may be able to prevent the parent state from regaining control. Given that territories that secede without consent of their parent states rarely gain international recognition, these rebellious territories are often left in an international legal and political limbo. While they may have been able to achieve effective independence, they cannot convert this into a formal place within the international system of states. Such a territory then becomes what is generally known as a de facto state. (Confusingly, other terms are sometimes used for such territories, such as "unrecognized states" or "contested states.") A de facto state is therefore best defined as an entity that has the key attributes of statehood, is not a member of the UN, and has little or no international recognition.

In many cases, de facto states will exist (or persist) until a resolution of some sort is reached. Sometimes, the two parties—the parent state and the de facto state—will try to resolve the situation, either by negotiation leading to an official separation (an exceedingly rare outcome) or by agreeing to reunification in some form. Alternatively, a parent state may bide its time until it feels it can force the rebellious territory back under its control. However, such situations can last for many years, if not decades. For example, the Turkish Republic of Northern Cyprus unilaterally declared independence in 1983; Somaliland has existed as a de facto state since 1991; and Abkhazia and Transnistria, which emerged with the collapse of the Soviet Union, are in their fourth decades of existence as de facto states.

What is a failed state?

A failed state, sometimes known as a "quasi-state," is a country that is generally recognized by the international community but has lost the key component of a government with effective control of its territory and population. It exists as a territory with a population but without functioning administration. Therefore, while failed states are members of the UN and other international institutions and can even sign treaties and nominally continue to carry out regular diplomatic relations, they are incapable of governing more than a fraction of their citizens and territory effectively. (In many ways, a failed state can be thought of as the exact opposite of a de facto state. A failed state is recognized as a state but cannot act as such. A de facto state has the attributes of statehood but is not recognized.) Perhaps the best example of a failed state in modern times is Somalia, which collapsed as a state in the early 1990s.

Failed states have become a deep source of concern to the international community because they often become sources of extreme poverty and deprivation. They are also more prone to ethnic and other civil conflicts, as well as serious human rights violations. All this can lead to refugee outflows as people try to escape. More recently, the lack of effective—and sometimes any—governance has led to piracy and provided a haven for terrorist groups. All these factors can have a huge effect on neighboring countries, as well as on the international system as a whole.

The sources of state failure are varied. In nearly all cases it is marked by the collapse or substantial shrinkage of central government authority, often following a widely contested election, or by some sort of rebellion. Interestingly, failed states are largely a product of the post-colonial period. While prior to decolonization there certainly had been governments unable to maintain effective control for an extended period, this was a relatively unusual occurrence. Sovereignty presupposed effectiveness. Governments incapable of establishing or maintaining effective control risked external intervention. However, in the period of post-1945 decolonization, the prior requirement of effective control was largely abandoned. If territories had an international legal right to independence, then they were given statehood and their existence had to be respected, irrespective of their internal conditions. Moreover, they continued to exist and be recognized as states even if they could no longer carry out the basic functions of statehood.

What is the difference between a micro-state and a micro-nation?

One issue that sometimes comes up is the difference between a micro-state and micro-nations. While they may appear to be similar, and some news organizations might incorrectly use them interchangeably, they are in fact rather different from each other.

A "microstate" is a territory that meets the attributes of statehood, and is a member of the UN, but has a very small population or territory. Microstates include countries such as Monaco, San Marino, Liechtenstein, some Caribbean states, and many of the South Pacific Island states. As noted earlier, there are around 15 countries with fewer than 100,000 inhabitants.

In contrast, a "micro-nation" is a term used to describe a territory that has "declared independence"—often at the whim of an eccentric "ruler"—but does not meet the generally accepted criteria for statehood, such as a settled population or effective governance. Perhaps the most famous micro-nation is the Principality of Sealand. This was founded in 1967 on an abandoned concrete naval fortress off the east coast of the UK in an attempt to bypass its restrictive radio broadcast laws. More recently, there was a flurry of interest in the establishment of The Republic of Liberland on an island in the Danube River between Serbia and Croatia. Although amusing, these entities are not states in any real sense—even if they may adopt certain trappings of statehood, such as choosing a flag and an anthem and issuing stamps. They certainly have no hope of gaining international recognition.

2

OLD RULES

SECESSION AND STATE CREATION, 1776–1945

When did modern states emerge?

States, as we now understand them, began to emerge in Europe in the first half of the sixteenth century in a process closely tied to the rise of the Reformation in Western Christianity and the appearance of the concept of state sovereignty.

During the Middle Ages, the European political and legal system was essentially vertical. All political entities within Western Christianity saw themselves as subordinate to the ultimate authority of the Pope, the head of the medieval Christian Church. With the rapid spread of Protestantism, a principal plank of which was the rejection of papal authority, the medieval system started to crumble. Beginning with Sweden, in 1527, and England, in 1534, Protestant rulers declared themselves to be the supreme authority within their territories. This led to a long series of wars as the Papacy and its allies challenged the Protestant claims of sovereignty.

By the middle of the seventeenth century, the European political and legal landscape had been largely transformed. The vertical system of medieval Western Christendom had been supplanted by a horizontal system dominated by sovereign states, as even Catholic rulers became attracted to the idea of full control over their lands. The most important symbolic milestone in the demise of the medieval European system was the Peace of Westphalia (1648). This peace ended the Thirty Years' War, the last conflict in a century of Protestant-Catholic wars, and is now regarded as the start of the modern era.

How did recognition develop?

As a result of the Reformation and the Peace of Westphalia, Europe had become a multitude of separate states that accepted one another's independence not merely as a matter of fact but also as a matter of right. Likewise, when new countries emerged, they not only claimed independence against the state they were leaving but also against other existing states. This anarchic and decentralized international system drove the need to devise an institutional method to assess the validity of claims of statehood by these new entities. That procedure became known as recognition. It was the way in which existing states certified that a new country possessed all the rights and obligations associated with sovereign statehood in the new international system.

How did the independence of the United States of America shape state creation?

The creation of the United States of America in 1776 has an absolutely central place in the story of statehood and recognition.

In terms of the internal political development of states, the United States was the first country that explicitly proclaimed that legitimate government should be based on the consent of the governed, that it should be designed to protect the rights inherent in human beings, and that it should be limited in its authority by a constitutional separation of powers. Prior to this, most states were absolutist hereditary monarchies. According to the principle of the divine right of kings, the dynastic lineage had a religious claim to authority. In principle, this meant that the monarchical right to rule was unlimited—even if the royal prerogative was often constrained by the nobility, cities, or other segments of society. This idea of monarchical authority was difficult to shake off, even in countries which had formally rejected it. For example, at the time of US independence, both Great Britain, formally a parliamentary monarchy, and the Netherlands, formally a republic, had relatively strong hereditary rulers and weak legislatures. In contrast, the US liberal model of a rights-protecting constitutional republic founded on popular will would prove, directly or indirectly, to be extremely influential to others experiencing different forms of arbitrary rule. Many constitutional systems around the world have sought to mirror US founding documents—principally the US Declaration of Independence and the US Constitution—or practices.

The creation of the United States was also significant in terms of the development of the relations between states. First, the emergence of the United States, the only generally recognized new state in the eighteenth century, demonstrated that foreign recognition of a new state is a necessary precondition of its external existence as a state. While the mid-seventeenth century saw the recognition of Swiss, Dutch, and Portuguese independence, these cases—which occurred while the modern states system was itself being formed, and while existing entities were gradually accepting each other's sovereignty irrespective of whether their rulers' religious denomination was Protestant or Catholic—did not establish a standardized recognition practice. New aspirants for statehood were a rarity and those that emerged, such as Corsica and Crimea, did not establish themselves securely or long enough to appeal for broad international recognition. In contrast, once the United States declared independence, its leaders sought recognition from major as well as minor foreign powers. (Among the first countries to recognize the United States were Morocco and Sweden.) In doing so, they clearly understood that without recognition the United States would be excluded from enjoying the rights associated with statehood internationally, including the rights to have open and regular diplomatic and economic relations and to conclude interstate treaties and agreements.

Second, the admission of the United States into the system of states clarified the criteria of legitimate statehood. Unable to rely on established practice or recent precedents for guidance, the overwhelming majority of existing states saw the unilateral secession of the thirteen colonies as being at odds with dynastic rights (this was largely a synonym for state rights, given the makeup of international society at that time). Dynastic rights, which reflected the theory of the divine right of kings, made the dominion of a legitimate monarchy inalienable. The only valid method of changing title to sovereignty or territory, and hence the only way a new state could be recognized, was through the consent of the affected monarch. This meant that the clear majority of existing states refused to recognize the United States until the British crown indicated it would do so, in peace talks with US negotiators in 1782. Interestingly, the sole exception was France. The French government disputed the applicability of dynastic rights to the creation of new states and instead recognized the United States in 1778 on what it claimed was the proper basis of de facto or effective statehood going back to recognition of the Netherlands, Switzerland, and Portugal. However, this was very much the minority view. No other states accepted the US claim that the thirteen colonies were entitled to dissolve their bonds with the parent state on their own accord—in other words, by revolution—and the French claim that an effectively established independent entity constituted a legitimate state internationally. A permanent population, a defined territory, a government, and even effective independence were not sufficient to acquire legitimate statehood: a component of an existing state required the consent of that state's sovereign. However novel or revolutionary an entity the United States was in terms of its internal system of government, it eventually managed to secure such consent.

How did Latin America gain independence?

After the United States became independent, the next wave of new states on the international stage were the countries of Latin America. Although the emergence of these states in the first half of the nineteenth century had complex and varied roots, in most cases it was linked to the period of Napoleonic rule in France and the Iberian Peninsula.

The second country in the Americas to achieve statehood after the United States was Haiti, in 1804, following a slave rebellion against their French overlords. This was followed by the independence of the Spanish and Portuguese colonies. Having essentially ruled themselves during the Napoleonic era, when Spain was under French rule, they had no wish to come under restored autocratic monarchical rule from a distant metropolitan state. Starting in 1811, and extending over a period of around fifteen years, the Spanish American territories—including Ecuador, Colombia, Mexico, Paraguay, Venezuela, Chile, Argentina, Bolivia—unilaterally seceded from the Spanish crown.

However, the great continental European powers, which continued to support the principle of dynastic legitimacy, insisted that they should not be recognized. Some even went so far as to threaten military intervention to help restore Spanish rule. In contrast, the United States and the UK—which since the early 1790s had undergone a series of constitutional reforms that had weakened the monarchy—took a very different view. As the leading lights of classical liberal thinking, the two countries argued that each people had a natural right to determine their political destiny, including a right to renounce the sovereign authority under which they lived. In effect, this became a precursor of what would later be known as the right to self-determination. They also believed that third parties had an obligation not to interfere in this process, as doing so would violate the principle of non-intervention in the domestic affairs of a foreign state.

According to the UK and the United States, the requirement for third parties to abstain from intervening in the self-determination process necessarily meant that they should also respect its outcome, whichever way it turned out. If a people managed to secure effective statehood—seen as the formation of a stable, effective territorial entity in which the population habitually obeyed the new rulers—then they deserved to have that reality on the ground recognized. As there was no international agreement on a valid method of assessing popular will, any outside assessment was to be based on the presumption that the de facto state was the embodiment of, in the words of Thomas Jefferson, "the will of the nation substantially declared." In other words, it was assumed that neither the establishment, nor the continued existence, of a de facto state was possible without at least tacit approval by its inhabitants. This presumption of popular consent, which trumped previous notions of dynastic consent, led the United States and the UK to conclude that states that had proven their de facto existence should be recognized. As they saw it, the duty to respect Spain's sovereignty and territorial integrity in the Americas depended on Spanish America being in Spanish hands. The displacement of the parent country by a self-determined de facto state extinguished that obligation. The United States proclaimed this new policy in an 1823 presidential address to the US Congress which later became known as the Monroe Doctrine. The UK announced the policy through the less well known Polignac Memorandum the same year.

Why was Latin American independence so significant?

The independence of the countries of Latin America marked the next stage in the evolution of international attitudes toward independence and statehood. It was significant for three key reasons. For a start, it marked a decisive blow to the principle of dynastic rights, which had shaped the attitudes of almost all states to the recognition of the United States several decades earlier. Second, as noted earlier, it also represented the moment when the standard of effective, or de facto, statehood emerged. This standard would guide responses to secession for the next century and a half.

But perhaps the most important effect of the emergence of states in Latin America was the development of the principle of *uti possidetis juris*. Deriving from Roman property law *(uti possidetis, ita possidetis,* "as you possess, so you may possess"), it essentially meant that, unless relevant parties agree otherwise, the administrative boundaries of a territory prior to its independence would be recognized as its international borders once it became a state. In a modified form, the principle has become a core element of modern state creation because it usually, though by no means always, provides a straightforward mechanism for defining the territory of new states.

The principle emerged because of the relatively swift advent of more than a dozen new states in Latin America. This brought many jurisdictional problems because of the way in which Spain had organized its colonial holdings between higher colonial jurisdictions (vice-royalties) and lower ones (captaincies-general and others). The political identities and loyalties of inhabitants were attached to the lesser units, and it was these units that declared independence. However, in several instances, independence movements in vice-royal capitals claimed the territory of a lesser unit that had once been under its authority. For example, the authorities in Buenos Aires, the former metropolis of the Vice-Royalty of the Rio de la Plata, and the capital of the newly heralded United Provinces of the Rio de la Plata, not only controlled what would eventually become Argentina but also claimed the jurisdictions of Charcas (later Bolivia), Paraguay, and the Banda Oriental (later Uruguay).

If not addressed, these claims could have led to widespread conflict. To forestall this, the leaders of the newly formed republics gradually agreed to accept all political communities that managed to establish themselves as de facto independent within the administrative divisions drawn by the Spanish crown, without regard for their previous standing in the hierarchy of Spanish colonial law. In other words, where loyalties had not existed at the level of vice-royalties, the lesser administrative boundaries delineated by Spain were followed. To this end, *uti possidetis juris* did not determine which units were eligible for sovereign status. Rather, it determined that once they had established themselves as de facto states, they were to inherit whatever borders they had under colonial law and were not entitled to territory beyond them or to be subsumed under what may have previously been higher-level entities. The emergence of the principle of *uti possidetis juris* in Latin America was therefore designed to safeguard newly established states against territorial conquest by their neighbors.

How did the US Civil War shape attitudes to secession?

The international response to the secession of southern states from the United States and their establishment of the Confederate States of America in 1861 is a very good example of the practical effects of the norms of statehood and recognition established in Latin America some forty years earlier. The central issue in sometimes tense diplomacy between the United States and other powers, especially the UK and France, was whether the Confederate States of America had become conclusively established as a de facto state.

Following years of fierce disputes over slavery, and starting in December 1860 with South Carolina, several southern states declared independence. While they claimed that the US Constitution gave US states a right of unilateral secession, the federal government denied that any such right existed. As soon as it came to power, the new administration of Abraham Lincoln tried to influence the way foreign states behaved toward the Confederate States of America, which had been proclaimed in February 1861. Even before active hostilities broke out, US Secretary of State William Seward pleaded with the British, the most important outside power in the Americas, for external non-intervention in the internal conflict. But even he admitted that other foreign powers would be within their right to recognize the Confederated States if they conclusively proved their existence as an independent entity.[1]

Although they recognized the belligerency of the Confederacy, the UK, France, and other powers nevertheless declared neutrality in the struggle and accepted de facto statehood as the standard for full state recognition. But, crucially, they appeared to set a high threshold for such recognition and did not rush into any decision. Even after the major Confederate victories in the early phase of the civil war, when it appeared that the Union might not be able to subdue the secession, they held off recognition, preferring to wait and see. In all instances Confederate victories were indeed followed by Confederate setbacks and once the Union won decisive battles at Gettysburg and Vicksburg, in July 1863, the issue of recognition never resurfaced again.

How did state creation evolve in the second half of the nineteenth century?

The principle of de facto statehood that had emerged at the time of Latin American independence and had played a part in shaping international responses during the US Civil War, continued to play a crucial part in framing attitudes to secession over the course of the rest of the nineteenth century and the first part of the twentieth century. Specifically, the American and British view that effective control should be a central criterion for recognition came to be gradually accepted by other

---

1. As Seward stated, external states "may, and even ought, to recognize a new state which has absolutely and beyond question effected its independence, and permanently established its sovereignty" and that "a recognition in such a case affords no just cause of offence to the government of the country from which the new state has so detached itself." Secretary of State Seward to US Minister in Great Britain Adams, Department of State, Washington, April 10, 1861.

powers. While the decline of dynastic legitimacy and the rise of constitutional governments was a major reason for this shift, the concept of de facto statehood was undoubtedly helped by the fact that it offered the practical advantage of making the authorities in secessionist areas responsible for externally harmful acts, such as piracy, emanating from the territories under their control.

As a result, in the decades that followed, the attainment of de facto statehood would prove to be a fundamental component in the creation of new states. For example, it proved indispensable in cases of unilateral secession, such as the declaration of independence of Texas from Mexico (1836), Panama from Colombia (1903), and the Baltic republics from Russia (1917–1922). It was also applied to other internally driven changes to existing states, such as the merger of several states to form the Kingdom of Italy (1859–1861) and the dissolution of Austria-Hungary into several new states at the end of the First World War. It was even applied in cases involving peoples without prior juridical status or geographic boundaries, such as the creation of the Kingdom of Greece (1821–1832). And even though the concept of de facto statehood no longer forms the foundation for state creation and recognition practices—as will be seen, it has now been replaced by a general preference for respecting the territorial integrity of established states—the principle has occasionally been felt even in more recent times. Perhaps the best example in the post–Second World War era was the establishment of Israel after the end of the British mandate (1948–1949). Having survived an attack by its Arab neighbors, Israel's existence came to be widely accepted.

How did the principle of self-determination emerge?

One of the most influential ideas on secession and state creation came at the end of the First World War when US President Woodrow Wilson outlined the principle that peoples should have a right to rule themselves within their own nation states.

Not only did this represent a major shift in how the right to independence was viewed at the time, but its effects are still felt to this day. Even now, people talk about a right of self-determination leading to statehood. But, despite its significance, the principle put forward by Wilson had several serious shortcomings.

The principle of recognizing de facto statehood that had emerged during the nineteenth century meant that self-determination was essentially understood in negative terms. Third parties were obliged not to intervene in secessionist efforts. They were merely expected to recognize the result. If a territory managed to successfully establish an independent existence, then it should be accepted. In contrast, Wilson suggested that peoples had the right to self-determination. This meant that third parties had a positive obligation to help them reach this goal. He wanted the United States, and other countries, to be active champions of those yearning for statehood. As he put it, he hoped to liberate "men who never could have liberated themselves."[2]

While the policy appeared laudable in principle, it raised important practical questions. First, which peoples would qualify for the right of self-determination? Secondly, what would be the appropriate procedure for assessing their will to be independent? Thirdly, what would be the exact scope of international support owed to them? None of these questions had obvious answers. For example, regarding who would qualify for self-determination, it was unclear whether the right of self-determination should be recognized for any group that merely called for independence, or whether it required some form of action. In none of his famous speeches did Wilson suggest that

2. Woodrow Wilson, "Appeal for Support of the League of Nations at Pueblo, Colorado," in Mario R. DiNunzio (editor), *Woodrow Wilson: Essential Writings and Speeches of the Scholar President* (New York: New York University Press, 2006), p. 412.

an active effort to pursue statehood should be a prerequisite for support.

On top of this, there were the very real practical problems associated with the policy. How could claims to self-determination be assessed as genuinely representative if they were, in nearly all cases, disputed? And how could outside states ensure the fulfilment of self-determination claims if the people claiming self-determination were not actually in possession of the territory they claimed? For example, if the Irish people had a right to self-determination and clearly wanted independence from British rule, as an Irish delegation told Wilson in October 1918, was it then the responsibility of the United States and other foreign states to dislodge the UK from Ireland? Taken together, these questions presented profound, if not insurmountable, operational difficulties.

These difficulties became apparent during the Paris Peace Conference at the end of the First World War. By the end of the conference, participants, including Wilson himself, recognized that if the mere voicing of a wish for statehood gave groups a positive entitlement to independence, and that if outsiders were then bound to intervene to support such claims, there would be no limit to state fragmentation and international disorder. For these reasons, whatever Wilson's rhetoric on self-determination, his ideas in fact came to very little in the aftermath of the First World War. Only Czechoslovakia, Poland, Yugoslavia, Finland, and the Baltic republics, which had attained de facto independent statehood, received international recognition. Many other peoples, such as the Kurds, failed to secure a state, despite their stated wish to do so.

Therefore, while the idea of self-determination put forward by Wilson was ground-breaking in theory, its practical impact on international practice was in fact delayed for decades. The notion of the right to self-determination only came to partial fruition after 1945, with the process of decolonization.

How were the Montevideo criteria for statehood developed?

As noted in Chapter 1, the Montevideo Convention on the Rights and Duties of States is now deemed to define the fundamental conditions of statehood. Indeed, it has come to be seen by many as a hallowed text. However, while the criteria are often cited by international lawyers, the details of the convention are not actually particularly well known. For example, few are aware that it was an inter-American, rather than a global, treaty.

The convention, which was formally signed on December 26, 1933, was initiated by Latin American jurists and governments to put in place a legally binding treaty to underpin Franklin Delano Roosevelt's anti-interventionist Good Neighbor Policy toward Latin America. Formulated upon his inauguration, in March 1933, the policy was designed to do away with three decades of US interference in the domestic affairs of Latin American countries. This interference included the unilateral non-recognition and sanctioning of de facto governments that the United States deemed had been formed "illegitimately," for example by military coups or other constitutionally irregular methods. This explains the inclusion of Article 3, which states that, "The political existence of the state is independent of recognition by the other states." This line is now—incorrectly—cited by many international legal scholars as proof that statehood does not require recognition. However, when read in its proper context, the text of the convention suggests a very different meaning. It was in fact explicitly designed to reinforce the principle of legal equality of states and to delegitimize various forms of foreign interference in the Americas, including the refusal to recognize an indigenously established de facto state.

More generally, given that its principal purpose was to regulate relations between American states, the convention was not designed to be the first or last word on statehood. It did not spell out fully what the criteria of acquisition of statehood had been historically. Nor did it stipulate that if an entity met the criteria of statehood it automatically possessed the rights of a state internationally even without recognition—as many mistakenly believe. As shown, the provision on recognition was intended to be read in a very different way. For this reason, there is a very good argument to be made that the Montevideo criteria are given more significance than they rightfully deserve.

How did the principle of the territorial integrity of states emerge?

One of the most important principles of modern international politics is that the acquisition of territory by force by a state should not be internationally accepted. For much of history, international politics was essentially shaped by "might is right." Whichever side prevailed in a given situation would be the winner. If a country managed to conquer a territory of another country in an armed conflict, it had a right to acquire it. However, this "right to conquest" began to change in the interwar period.

Originally known as the Stimson Doctrine, the doctrine of non-recognition originated from two main sources. The first was Article 10 of the League of Nations Covenant (1919). This obliged members to protect and to preserve all members' territorial integrity against external aggression. The second was the Pact of Paris (1928), better known as the Kellogg-Briand Pact. Originally signed by fifteen states—including the United States, the UK, France, Germany, and Japan—with a further forty following later, the pact outlawed war as an instrument of national policy.

The doctrine was formulated following Japan's invasion and occupation of the Chinese province of Manchuria, in 1931. As Japan consolidated its control of the province, US Secretary of State Henry Stimson announced, in January 1932, that the United States did not "intend to recognize any situation, treaty or agreement which may be brought about by means contrary to the covenants and obligations of the Pact of Paris of 27 August 1928, to which treaty both China and Japan, as well as the United States, are parties." As the United States had not ratified the League of Nations Covenant, and was not a member of the organization, the declaration was merely a unilateral statement of Washington's views. However, it gained significance when, a few weeks later, the League of Nations Council, adding a reference to Article 10, made non-recognition a policy that all members "ought" to follow. As a result, the subsequent declaration of an independent State of Manchukuo was not initially recognized by any country other than Japan. (Although, in the context of the descent toward the Second World War, it was later recognized by Italy, Spain, Germany, Hungary, and the Soviet Union.) The League of Nations and the United States both rejected Japanese assertions that Manchukuo was the outcome of authentic, internal self-determination. As they saw it, the entity could not have been established without external force and was, therefore, unlawful.

The application of the Stimson Doctrine to the case of Manchukuo highlighted several important legal and political developments regarding secession and state creation. Statehood could not be understood simply as the sum of the criteria laid down by the Montevideo Convention. It could not be acquired in violation of existing norms of international law. Additionally, although the Montevideo Convention claimed that statehood was not dependent on recognition, in truth a general lack of recognition meant that an entity did not exist as a state in international relations and law in practical terms. But perhaps most importantly, it showed that the criteria of statehood, and consequently the terms of recognition, could evolve as broader international attitudes changed.

This would be graphically highlighted following the end of the Second World War. The practice of non-recognition of legal claims arising out of forcible territorial change was not only re-established, it was also given an added emphasis in the new international order that emerged. Most notably, the territorial integrity of states was implicitly recognized in Article 2(4) of the Charter of the United Nations, which prohibits the threat or use of force against the territory or political independence of any state. This was subsequently confirmed in a wide range of other global and regional treaties and legal texts, such as the UN Friendly Relations Declaration and the Helsinki Final Act, which led to the eventual creation of the Organization for Security and Cooperation in Europe. The idea of territorial integrity now forms a central pillar of the international system.

3

MODERN RULES

SELF-DETERMINATION AND DECOLONIZATION, 1945–1990

How did decolonization begin?

In the context of secession and state creation, the most mo-mentous trend to emerge after the Second World War was the process of decolonization. By the end of the war, there was a growing understanding outside of Europe that colonialism had no place in the modern world. That said, there was still a general view in international circles that overseas colonialism was a necessary international institution until the colonies had attained full "civilization" and could demonstrate an ability to run their own independent governments effectively. This nine-teenth- and early twentieth-century view was even reflected in the charter of the newly established UN. Chapter XI of the UN Charter, the "Declaration Regarding Non-Self-Governing Territories," called on relevant members "to assist them in the progressive development of their free political institutions."

While decolonization arrived as early as the 1940s for some countries—such as India, Palestine, Burma (now more usually known as Myanmar), and Indonesia—it was over the course of the 1950s that calls for independence really gathered pace, and it became clear that a systematic approach to the issue was needed. By the mid-1950s, the assumption that sovereignty presupposed "civilization" was under wholesale assault. Even the colonial powers themselves were increasingly unable to mount a credible defense in the face of calls for decolonization. A near universal consensus developed in international society that colonial rule and dependent status were no longer admissible. Decolonization documents for the first time proclaimed that "all peoples have the right to self-determination" and that all colonial peoples wishing for independence must be allowed to attain it, regardless of any deficiencies in the political, social, economic, or educational conditions of their territories. From there the process of decolonization moved swiftly. In the ten years between 1955 and 1965, membership of the UN almost doubled, from 60 to 117. (A full list of UN members, and when they joined, can be found in Appendix A.)

Why was the process of decolonization so significant?

Decolonization was transformative in several interrelated ways. First, it represented a triumph for the Wilsonian positive-right conception of self-determination. UN General Assembly Resolution 1514 (1960),[1] the landmark document of decolonization, for the first time defined specific peoples—the peoples of the non-self-governing and trust territories (the latter being the successors to League of Nations mandates)—as being entitled to statehood. The resolution made it clear that if the populations of these UN Charter–designated colonial territories voiced their desire for independence, then the colonial power was required to withdraw, and third parties should help facilitate the emergence of a new state in their place. Decolonization therefore appeared to answer the key questions that eluded Wilson and his supporters: who specifically bears the right to self-determination and independence, and what are the obligations of third parties with respect to that right?

1. "Declaration on the Granting of Independence to Colonial Countries and Peoples," UN General Assembly Resolution 1514, December 14, 1960.

While a few colonial powers refused initially to withdraw from at least some of their territories, they all eventually came to accept decolonization. (Portugal and South Africa held out longest.) As a result, the process was in fact relatively peaceful. While there were certainly notable cases where colonial powers fought what were often brutal conflicts against self-determinations movements—for example, the campaigns by France in Algeria and Vietnam, the Netherlands in Indonesia, Portugal in Mozambique and Angola, and Britain in Kenya and Cyprus—most colonial independence processes in fact occurred without direct violence.

Second, decolonization transformed the criteria of statehood and recognition. The international community largely abandoned the criteria of effective statehood as the basis for recognizing indigenously founded new states. This did not necessarily mean that the countries being recognized lacked effectiveness. It merely meant that having a fully effective government was not considered to be a prerequisite of recognition. If an entity was considered entitled to self-determination, a nominal government was sufficient for recognition of statehood. Likewise, the notion that meeting the criteria of effective statehood qualifies a territory for foreign acknowledgment as a state—and that falling short excluded it from such acknowledgment—was effectively discarded.

How were the borders of the newly independent states decided?

One of the key issues arising from the process of decolonization was the definition of the borders of the new states. There were two distinct problems. The first related to the protection of the boundaries of the new state from neighboring states. The second related to fears that these new countries would face pressures from internal groups seeking either to secede or unite territory with neighboring states.

Ultimately, both questions were resolved by applying the long-standing principle of *uti possidetis juris*, which, as we saw in Chapter 2, had first emerged at the time of Latin American independence. It was agreed that the territorial boundaries set by colonial powers would remain in force and would not be subject to change without the agreement of the new state. Interestingly, the use of the principle of *uti possidetis* to protect a state against domestic threats was in fact a novel conceptual innovation. In the nineteenth century, the principle was used to safeguard the territory of new states against external depredations and not against internal acts of secession. For example, it did not grant protection to Mexico or Colombia against the secession of Texas and Panama. Internationally, those acts fell under the regular recognition criteria of de facto statehood. In contrast, with post-1945 decolonization, the principle also came to be understood as protecting the rights of newly formed states against internal challenges to their sovereignty and territorial integrity. At the instant of independence, the borders of the new state would become sacrosanct. They would not be subject to change either by external force or by internal insurrection.

Although this appeared to be a sensible approach, it was in fact problematic. Most colonial boundaries were artificial— and often strikingly so. Imperial powers had delineated and imposed them without regard for pre-colonial political systems and without input from native inhabitants. In Latin America these frontiers had crystallized over time into lines of political demarcation—by the time of the wars of independence in the early nineteenth century they contained, for the most part, populations with distinct and developed national consciousness. In Africa, Asia, and the South Pacific, though, colonial borders often failed to correspond to actual patterns of political allegiance. *Uti possidetis juris* therefore did little to produce a unified citizenry within the new international borders. Many communities within and across the newly minted interstate frontiers, usually self-defined in ethno-cultural terms, claimed the right of self-determination against the countries they found themselves in. However, their ambitions were thwarted as the borders of the state they now lived in were deemed to be inviolable.

How were the principles of self-determination and territorial integrity reconciled?

One of the greatest tensions in modern international relations concerns the apparent right of peoples to self-determination and the right of states to have their territorial integrity respected. How could the international community recognize the right of people to have their own state when they were simultaneously obliged to recognize the borders of existing states? To solve this conundrum, the concept of self-determination came to be understood in two very different ways.

The first of these is what is known as "external self-determination." This form of self-determination permitted a people to pursue independent statehood. However, it came to be understood in relation to a very narrow set of circumstances. Primarily, it applied to overseas colonies and territories considered to be under external subjugation, such as occupied land. It also came to be accepted that it applied to new states established by agreement—either an agreement with other constituent units of consensually dissolved states, such as the Mali Federation, which led to the creation of Mali and Senegal in 1960, or with the agreement of the parent state in the case of seceding entities.

Crucially, the right to external self-determination was not deemed to allow the non-consensual secession from the territory of a state. This was important as this was historically the most common method of state formation. Self-determination claims from within newly decolonized territories, as well as long-standing states, became routinely opposed by the international community because they violated the territorial integrity of the parent state. Instead, in these cases, a second form of self-determination emerged. This was the concept of an "internal" self-determination. Rather than self-determination leading to independence, this was understood as a right of peoples to political participation within the state, for example through territorial autonomy or self-rule in specific areas, such as education and culture. This was seen to be justified because peoples living in existing states, as opposed to colonial or externally subjugated territories, had already had a right to independence realized.

There were several reasons why states adopted this approach. Most obviously, it was the result of concerns about the domino effect of never-ending secessionist bids arising from the rapidly growing number of new states, many of which had ethnically mixed populations. However, there were also fears of violence and instability arising from conflicting claims of statehood within a given territory. Such concerns were fed by the history of failure to resolve past disputes between antagonistic majorities and minorities through territorial partitions or border changes, as had happened in Ireland, Palestine, and India. Lastly, there was a clear preference by the overwhelming majority of governments for an inclusive civic conception of the nation. In their view, the state should represent all citizens of a territory. It should not be based on an exclusive ethnic conception of nationhood that represented just one group—a conception that, especially in the post–Second World War period, evoked Nazi projects for ethnic or racial purity.

The new rules governing self-determination, secession, and recognition were largely respected by states and international organizations in the years that followed. The only post-colonial sub-state entity that was able to establish an internationally legitimate state following a unilateral secession was Bangladesh. (The reasons behind this will be examined later.) However, the desire for self-determination leading to statehood among various peoples persisted. The number of secessionist bids, often accompanied by violence, would rise sharply in the following decades.

When did unilateral secession become so unacceptable?

Although there had always been a disquiet about the destabilizing potential of unilateral secession, throughout the nineteenth and early twentieth centuries it was generally accepted that if a territory had effectively attained de facto statehood it should be recognized. However, this all changed in the period of decolonization. Interestingly, this did not occur quite as soon, or as quickly, as many might imagine.

In real terms, the emergence of contemporary hostility to unilateral secession can be traced back to two cases of separatism that occurred in Africa in the 1960s. Katanga's attempt to break away from the Democratic Republic of the Congo and Biafra's attempt to secede from Nigeria marked the start of the international community's practice of opposing unilateral secession. With these cases, the principle of respecting the territorial integrity of states no longer applied just to threats from other countries. Henceforth, it would also be applied to internal attempts to secede.

On July 1, 1960, the Republic of Congo (now known as the Democratic Republic of Congo) gained independence from its colonial power, Belgium, and immediately descended into chaos. Ten days later, Katanga, the wealthiest of the new country's six provinces, unilaterally declared independence. Unable to attain effective control over the country, the pro-Soviet Congolese government under Prime Minister Patrice Lumumba requested military help from the UN. On July 17, the UN Security Council established a peacekeeping operation, ONUC (Opération des Nations Unies au Congo).[2]

Although its mission was to stabilize the Congo, including by facilitating the withdrawal of all remaining Belgian troops still in the country, the Congolese government demanded that ONUC be deployed to defeat the Katanga secession efforts. UN Secretary-General Dag Hammarskjold refused. As he

2. UN Security Council Resolution 143, July 17, 1960.

saw it, the secessionist bid constituted an internal matter for the Congo—despite evidence showing that it was supported by Belgian, French, and UK mining interests. However, following Hammarskjold's death in a plane crash, in September 1961, the UN's view shifted. Although most of the other tasks assigned to the UN force, including overseeing the departure of all Belgian troops, had been completed, and although there was no longer evidence of external governmental involvement in the secession, the UN Security Council now concluded that one of its explicit tasks ought to be to safeguard the Congo against the loss of Katanga. UN Security Council Resolution 169 (1961) "completely" rejected Katanga's claim to sovereignty and declared all secessionist activities contrary to the Congolese constitution. UN forces were now deployed to defeat the Katanga secession. This was achieved in 1963.

The crucial aspect of the Katanga case was the high level of international agreement that eventually emerged on the need to quell the secession. This was driven by a range of very different considerations. For the Soviets, it was a wish to hold the country together in the hope that a united, pro-Soviet government may yet emerge, despite the assassination of Prime Minister Lumumba in 1961. Meanwhile, the United States feared that the loss of Katanga might have a "domino effect." It was particularly wary of the potential secession of another Congolese province, Orientale, which was led by a leftist, pro-Soviet politician. At the same time, many new states in the UN faced actual or potential separatist movements and therefore feared that Katanga's independence would encourage other secessionist efforts. Therefore, while there were very different reasons for opposing Katanga's attempt to break away, the result would be the emergence of a general opposition to unilateral secession everywhere.

This newfound opposition to secession was seen very clearly a few years later when in 1967 the Republic of Biafra unilaterally declared independence from Nigeria. Although the claim to statehood was based on the central government's violent oppression of the region's majority Igbo population, the secession was nevertheless condemned by most of the international community as a violation of Nigeria's territorial integrity. While a few states—such as Gabon, Haiti, Ivory Coast, Tanzania, and Zambia—recognized Biafra, most other countries called for a settlement based on Nigerian unity. Some states, including the Soviet Union and the United Kingdom, even went as far as to supply the Nigerian government with weapons to put down the rebellion. After a bloody civil war that is estimated to have left three million dead, Biafra's attempted secession ended in January 1970.

Biafra confirmed the general international opposition to unilateral secession, even when it was primarily an internally driven process free of direct external involvement. This represented a profound break with the approach in the nineteenth century, whereby domestic challenges to the territorial integrity of a state were a matter to be addressed internally. Outside statements in favor of an outcome were thought to compromise the right of a people to determine their government. Unless there were valid reasons to intervene, such as self-defense, outsiders were expected to leave conflicting claims of sovereignty to the test of effective control. Whichever side prevailed would then be accepted internationally. In contrast, the new approach whereby unilateral secession would be opposed in the name of territorial integrity opened the door for outsiders to intervene by a variety of means to maintain parent state unity. There can be little doubt that the overwhelming international support for the central governments in Congo and Nigeria contributed to failure of the efforts by Katanga and Biafra to secede.

Have there been any successful cases of unilateral secession since 1945?

Although the successful efforts to put down the attempted secessions by Katanga and Biafra signaled that the international community now put the territorial integrity of states before the self-determination of peoples, there was in fact an instance when unilateral secession did triumph. Bangladesh's independence from Pakistan just a few years later ostensibly suggested that it was still possible to secede without approval from a parent state under certain conditions.

When it became independent, in 1947, Pakistan was geographically divided into two parts, East and West Pakistan. These were separated by 1,300 miles of Indian territory. Although more populous, the east was politically dominated by the west. This created resentment. In 1970, the eastern autonomist party, the Awami League, won parliamentary elections. However, the western-dominated military government refused to accept the results. On March 26, 1971, East Pakistan unilaterally declared independence as the People's Republic of Bangladesh. Initially, the international community supported Pakistan's territorial integrity, despite the massive repression meted out by the Pakistani army in East Pakistan. However, events changed in December that year when India, which had received ten million refugees from East Pakistan, claimed to have been attacked by Pakistan. In retaliation, it joined the conflict and recognized Bangladesh.

Within days, India had defeated the Pakistani army, and thus brought an end to effective Pakistani authority in its eastern province. It was now unrealistic to expect that Pakistani sovereignty could be restored. Over the months that followed, with India withdrawing its troops and governance in the hands of the new Bangladeshi authorities, many states decided to recognize an independent Bangladesh. Most importantly, it was recognized by the Soviet Union, United States, France, and the UK. (Importantly, and in the context of the Cold War, the Soviet Union and the United States feared that Bangladesh would align with the other superpower if they did not recognize it.) By 1974, even Pakistan had accepted that its former eastern part was a lost cause and recognized it as an independent state. In September that year, Bangladesh became the 136th UN member.

While this could be read as proof that unilateral secession was still possible, history has since shown that this was in fact a unique case. No other territory has managed to receive widespread international recognition and then full UN membership after breaking away without the consent of the ex-colonial parent state. As shown, Bangladesh only achieved this because of an exceptional set of circumstances, including Pakistan's eventual decision to accept its statehood.

How has the UN reacted to unilateral acts of secession?

While there have been many cases of attempted secession since 1945, surprisingly few have ever come before the Security Council, the main UN body dealing with matters of international peace and security. Very often, parent states and the wider international community prefer to regard UDIs as internal matters and not give them greater international significance. For instance, and to use a relatively recent example, Spain did not bring Catalonia's UDI before the Security Council in 2017. In other cases, deadlock in the council makes any consideration of an act of unilateral secession impossible. A good case in point was Kosovo's 2008 UDI from Serbia, which was supported by three veto-wielding permanent members of the Security Council—the United States, the UK, and France. However, just occasionally, a UDI will come before the council. The 1983 UDI of the Turkish Republic of Northern Cyprus (TRNC), often referred to as Northern Cyprus, is a rare case in point.

In 1960, the island of Cyprus became independent after eighty years of UK colonial rule. A complex constitution was put in place that balanced political power between the island's Greek and Turkish Cypriot communities, representing 78 and 18 percent of the population respectively. (The remaining 4 percent was made up of three smaller religious communities.) However, just three years later this power-sharing system broke down and the island descended into conflict. In March 1964, the UN Security Council set up a peacekeeping mission on the island (UNFICYP) and established a mediation effort. Over the next decade, efforts to secure a political agreement between the two communities failed.

In July 1974, the Greek military government overthrew the Cypriot government as a prelude to annexing the island. In response, Turkey invaded and occupied the northern third of Cyprus. Despite this, the UN continued its peacemaking efforts between the two communities. In 1977, the two sides agreed that any future settlement should be based on a federal model. This was again confirmed by a second agreement in 1979. However, on November 15, 1983, the Turkish Cypriot leadership took advantage of political instability in Turkey and unilaterally declared independence—believing that this would strengthen their hand in negotiations. Although the Turkish government immediately recognized the so-called Turkish Republic of Northern Cyprus, the move was swiftly condemned by the UN Security Council. It declared the purported UDI to be invalid and called on member states not to recognize any state on the island other than the Republic of Cyprus.[3]

In this case, the UN Security Council became involved because the UDI took place in a country where there was an active UN peacekeeping and peacemaking mission and because the act of secession represented a direct challenge to the principles of a settlement that had been agreed by the parties and endorsed by the Security Council.

Why was Rhodesia's UDI so unusual?

Another very important case where the UN Security Council became involved was following Rhodesia's UDI in 1965. This was especially interesting—and was also unique—because we tend to associate UDIs with secession. This was in fact a very different type of situation that centered on decolonization.

3. UN Security Council Resolution 541, November 18, 1983.

Situated in southern Africa, the mineral rich territory of Southern Rhodesia became a UK protectorate in the late nineteenth century. In 1922, a referendum held among the territory's 18,000 white settlers showed that they favored self-rule over the alternative of union with neighboring South Africa. The territory became a UK crown colony on October 1, 1923. In 1953, as calls for decolonization grew, it was incorporated into the Central African Federation, alongside the protectorates of Northern Rhodesia and Nyasaland. This came to an end on December 31, 1963. The following year, Nyasaland and Northern Rhodesia gained independence, becoming Malawi and Zambia. While Southern Rhodesia had also been due to become independent, tensions arose after the UK government insisted that it must do so under majority black African rule in accordance with UN General Assembly Resolution 1514, which stated that the right to self-determination applied to the entire population of a colonial territory "without any distinction as to race, creed or color." This was rejected by the white colonial community, which represented just 5 percent of the population. With London refusing to back down on its demands, the territory unilaterally declared independence as "Rhodesia" on November 11, 1965.

The international response to the UDI was swift and strong. For the UK, the move was nothing less than an act of rebellion. It was declared illegal. At the same time, the UN Security Council passed Resolution 216. As well as condemning the UDI, it called on states not to recognize the "illegal racist minority regime" and to refrain from giving it any assistance. In the years that followed, Rhodesia became largely isolated on the world stage. No countries recognized it—not even South Africa, which operated a racist apartheid system. Meanwhile, an armed insurgency, the Rhodesian Bush War, erupted pitting the government against the guerrilla forces of two anti-colonial political movements, the Zimbabwe African National Union (ZANU) and the Zimbabwe African People's Union (ZAPU). By the late 1970s, Rhodesia had become irreparably weakened.

The government had no choice but to accept the end of white minority rule. Following peace talks in London, Rhodesia became the Republic of Zimbabwe on April 18, 1980. It was admitted as the 153rd member of the UN on August 25 that year.

Rhodesia was a very special example of a UDI. In this case, it was not about a territory trying to secede from an existing state. Instead, it was about a colony declaring independence on its own terms. Rather than merely end British colonial rule, the declaration of independence was designed to perpetuate the political, social, and economic privilege of the country's small white community. By resolutely opposing the decision to form a state based on minority rule, the international community helped to define the inclusive and democratic scope of the right of self-determination.

Did all colonial territories become independent?

No. While decolonization saw the emergence of many new states across Africa, Asia, the Caribbean, and the South Pacific, there were a few instances where the independence process did not lead to independent statehood. In some cases, this was because the territory wanted to unite voluntarily with another country—an outcome permitted by UN General Assembly Resolution 1541 on decolonization. Examples include Singapore (Malaysia), British Somaliland (Somali Republic), and British Togoland (Ghana). At other times, independence was not an option because another country had a preexisting and internationally accepted territorial claim to the area. The best example of this came when the UK left Hong Kong, in 1997, and the territory was passed to China. However, in some cases, the path to independence was thwarted by neighboring countries, which saw decolonization as an opportunity to seize the territory in question. Two particularly good examples are East Timor and Western Sahara.

Lying at the far end of the Indonesian archipelago as it stretches toward the Pacific, the eastern part of the island of Timor was colonized by Portugal in the sixteenth century.

In 1974, Portugal withdrew from its colonies in Africa and Asia following a left-wing military coup. On November 28, 1975, the Revolutionary Front for an Independent East Timor (FRETILIN) declared independence. Indonesia, which had sovereignty over the west of the island, rejected the announcement. Just over a week later, it invaded and annexed the territory. Recognizing the "inalienable right" of self-determination for the people of East Timor, the UN General Assembly and Security Council rejected the move and called on Indonesia to withdraw.[4] It refused to do so. This led to an armed insurgency.

Although the UN opened talks between Indonesia and Portugal on the future of the territory in 1983, no agreement was reached. It was not until the military-led government fell in 1998 that the situation changed. On May 5, 1999, Indonesia reached an agreement with Portugal to allow the people of East Timor a vote on their future. On August 30 a referendum was held in which 78 percent supported independence. Although the result was greeted with violence by pro-Indonesian militias, the Indonesian government accepted the vote. Under Resolution 1272, the UN Security Council authorized the establishment of a transitional administration (UNTAET). A little over two years later, on May 20, 2002, East Timor declared independence under the name Timor-Leste. On September 27, 2002, it became the 191st member of the UN.

The other example is Western Sahara. This is a sparsely populated region of Northwest Africa originally colonized by Spain in 1884. In 1963, the UN determined that, as a colonial territory, it had a right to self-determination. However, it was also claimed by Morocco to the north and Mauritania to the south. In December 1974, the UN General Assembly requested an advisory opinion from the International Court of Justice on the matter. The following year, the court ruled that neither Morocco nor Mauritania had a sovereign claim to the territory and that

---

4. UN General Assembly Resolution 3485 (XXX), December 12, 1975, and
   UN Security Council Resolution 384, December 22, 1975.

the Sahrawi people should have the right to exercise their right of self-determination.[5] Despite this decision, Spain withdrew from the territory after reaching an agreement with Morocco and Mauritania that saw the former annex two-thirds of the territory, and the latter take the other third. In response, pro-independence forces, the Polisario Front, launched an armed uprising and on February 26, 1976, proclaimed the Sahrawi Arab Democratic Republic (SADR). Three years later, Mauritania withdrew from and renounced its claims on Western Sahara. However, Morocco remained and even assumed control of most of the area previously claimed by Mauritania. In 1985, the UN initiated a peacemaking mission. In 1991, it was agreed that a self-determination referendum would be held offering the inhabitants a choice between independence or being a part of Morocco. Although the deal was endorsed by the Security Council,[6] the vote has never taken place as the two sides have never agreed on who would be entitled to take part, despite several major initiatives to resolve the matter—most notably under the auspices of former US Secretary of State James Baker. To date, the issue remains at a stalemate. Meanwhile, Western Sahara is recognized by over forty members of the UN and is a member of the African Union.[7]

While East Timor eventually managed to gain independence, and join the UN, Western Sahara has yet to do so. These two cases show that although the international community may have recognized a right of independence for colonial territories, it was not always able to ensure that it was realized.

5. International Court of Justice, "Western Sahara," Advisory Opinion, October 16, 1975.
6. UN Security Council Resolution 690, April 29, 1991.
7. States that currently recognize Western Sahara include South Africa, Nigeria, Iran, Mexico, Cuba, Jamaica, Nicaragua, El Salvador, Honduras, as well as other recent UN members South Sudan and East Timor. Other states—such as India and Peru—have recognized it and then withdrawn or frozen the decision. Some countries, such as Mauritius, have even frozen or withdrawn recognition and then restored it.

4

CHANGING RULES?

SECESSION IN THE CONTEMPORARY ERA, 1990–

How did the end of the Cold War change secession and statehood?

The end of the Cold War marked a profound change to the international system that had emerged after the end of the Second World War. The end of the bipolarity between the United States and the Union of Soviet Socialist Republics (USSR), or Soviet Union, heralded a new era of international instability with the collapse of the latter, the disintegration of Yugoslavia, and the breakup of Czechoslovakia. And yet, at the same time, there was a degree of continuity. Many of the rules that had been developed during the period of decolonization remained in place. As a result, there are now a number of de facto states that have managed to break away from the control of a parent state but have little or no prospect of attaining full international recognition.

How did the Soviet Union break apart?

The end of the Cold War and the subsequent collapse of the Soviet Union brought about the fastest expansion of new states in the history of the UN. In total, fifteen UN member states emerged from the disintegration of the USSR. However, the

exact processes and underlying principles leading to the creation of these states differed widely.

The first states to emerge were the three Baltic republics—
Estonia, Latvia, and Lithuania. Technically, none of them was
in fact a new state. All of them had been independent countries during the first half of the twentieth century before being
invaded and annexed by the Soviet Union at the start of the
Second World War. For the next fifty years, they remained
under Soviet control. However, as the Soviet Union began to
weaken, at the end of the 1980s, pressure for independence
grew. Despite foreign statements against unilateral secession
from the USSR, each of them began to reassert their authority
by holding referendums on independence and passing legis-
lation strengthening their autonomy. On August 19, 1991, this
process came to a head when hardline elements in Moscow
attempted to overthrow the Soviet government. Although the
coup was quickly put down, the Baltic republics seized their
chance to reassert independence. This was almost immediately
welcomed by the United States and other Western states—
many of which noted that they had never ceased recognizing
their independence. Crucially, their statehood was also
recognized by the Soviet government. All three were admitted
to the UN on September 17, 1991.[1]

The coup also provided an opportunity for Ukraine and
Belarus to assert their statehood. Interestingly, both were already full members of the UN. In fact, as the Ukrainian
Soviet Socialist Republic and the Byelorussian Soviet Socialist
Republic, they were both founding members of the UN in
1945—even if they were merely proxies for the Soviet government. This meant they did not have to apply for membership. On August 24, 1991, Ukraine declared independence,
informing the UN of its changed circumstances and its new

1. UN General Assembly Resolutions 46/4, 46/5, and 46/6, September
17, 1991.

name. The next day, August 25, 1991, Belarus followed suit and declared independence.

Following the departure of the Baltic republics, Ukraine, and Belarus, the question was what would happen to the rest of the Soviet Union. Everything now hinged on the Russian Soviet Federative Socialist Republic, by far the largest part of the Soviet Union. Would it seek to hold what remained of the USSR together, or would it allow the other republics to proclaim independence as well? In the end, it did neither. On December 25, 1991, in the wake of an agreement with other republics to dissolve the USSR, it asserted independence as the Russian Federation. With the consent of the other remaining Soviet republics, it retained the Soviet seat at the UN. With this move, all that was left was for the nine remaining republics—Moldova, the three states of the Caucasus (Georgia, Armenia, and Azerbaijan), and the five Central Asian republics (Kazakhstan, Kyrgyzstan, Tajikistan, Turkmenistan, and Uzbekistan)—to declare independence. Most of them joined the UN on March 2, 1992. The exception was Georgia, which joined a few months later, on July 31.

Why did some Soviet territories not gain independence?

As well as the fifteen UN members that emerged following the breakup of the Soviet Union, several other territories claimed independence but have not been recognized or have received only limited recognition. Most notably, there are the four major de facto states. In Moldova, the Pridnestrovian Moldavian Republic (PMR), more commonly known as Transnistria, is a long sliver of territory that lies on the border with Ukraine and is wholly unrecognized. Then there are the breakaway territories of South Ossetia and Abkhazia, which are recognized by Russia and handful of other countries, such as Nicaragua, Venezuela, and Syria. There is also Nagorno-Karabakh, a predominantly ethnic Armenian territory in Azerbaijan, which is also wholly unrecognized.

Most recently, Russia sponsored the efforts by two provinces in Ukraine to break away. The Luhansk People's Republic and the Donetsk People's Republic were both proclaimed in 2014 following the outbreak of fighting in the predominantly Russian-speaking east of the country and then recognized by Russia in February 2022. Neither gained any significant traction on the international stage. Indeed, Russia's decision to recognize them was formally condemned by the UN General Assembly shortly after Moscow's invasion of Ukraine began.[2] Unlike the four breakaway territories cited above, neither met even the most basic criteria of statehood. Then there are several other territories that attempted to secede but have since been reintegrated into their parent states. The best example is Chechnya, which attempted to secede from the Russian Federation. (Several of these cases will be examined again later in this chapter.)

The reasons why these various territories have not been recognized as independent states is again down to the application of the decolonization principle of *uti possidetis juris*. As the USSR collapsed, the international community decided to recognize only the highest pre-independence territorial jurisdictions within the Soviet Union. The international community therefore accepted the legitimacy of the inherited borders of the Soviet federal republics—regardless of the will of the different populations living within those jurisdictions. Lower order units were expected to remain within the republics where they were situated prior to the country's disintegration. Unless and until any of these territories obtain the permission of their parent states to secede, it seems highly unlikely that their claim to statehood will gain general international acceptance.

2. UN General Assembly Resolution ES-11/1, March 2, 2022.

How did Yugoslavia disintegrate?

Unlike the collapse of the Soviet Union, which was by and large a peaceful process, the disintegration of Yugoslavia became the most serious armed conflict in Europe since the end of the Second World War. However, the breakup of Yugoslavia also served to reaffirm many of the accepted norms of secession and state creation, including *uti possidetis juris* inherited from decolonization.

Yugoslavia first emerged at the end of the First World War as the Kingdom of Serbs, Croats, and Slovenes—a political union between Serbia, Montenegro, and several territories that had previously been a part of the Austro-Hungarian Empire. Following the end of the Second World War, communist rule was established, and the country became a federation composed of six republics: Bosnia and Herzegovina, Croatia, Macedonia, Montenegro, Serbia, and Slovenia. Following the death of the country's communist leader, Josip Broz Tito, in 1980, political tensions grew and over the course of the next decade the country began to fracture.

Despite strong opposition from the Yugoslav federal government and large parts of the international community, which voiced support for Yugoslavia's territorial integrity, Slovenia and Croatia declared independence on June 25, 1991. After a short conflict, the federal Yugoslav government accepted Slovenia's independence. On the other hand, Croatia's independence sparked major fighting as the Serbian community in the republic refused to accept its independence. Instead, Croatia's Serbs unilaterally declared independence and formed the Republic of Serbian Krajina (RSK). This was supported by Serbia, the largest and most populous republic of Yugoslavia, which argued that under the Yugoslav constitution the right of self-determination was not in the hands of the six republics but lay instead with the six constituent nations of Yugoslavia—the Bosnian Muslims (later known as Bosniaks), Croats, Macedonians, Montenegrins, Serbs, and Slovenes. In other words, Serbia argued that Serbs living in the other republics should have the right to self-determination as members of a constituent nation.

These events left the international community divided. While some countries preached caution, others, notably Germany, were determined to recognize Slovenia and Croatia. To clarify the legal issues at stake, the European Union created a special arbitration commission led by a former president of the French Constitutional Council, Robert Badinter. In its first opinion, the Badinter Commission decided that, with four out of the six republics no longer committed to the federation, the issue was not one of secession as such. Instead, it argued that Yugoslavia was in the process of dissolution. The parent state would cease to exist and would be replaced by multiple new states. In its second opinion, the commission, invoking *uti possidetis juris* from decolonization, determined that the Serbian communities did not have a separate right of self-determination. Instead, they were entitled only to minority rights. Following on from this, the third opinion clarified that the internal boundaries of the republics within Yugoslavia should now became the external borders of the new states and could only change by agreement. In early 1992, EU members recognized the independence of Slovenia and Croatia. Then, a few months later, on March 3, 1992, Bosnia and Herzegovina also declared independence. Again, the Serb community countered with their own declaration of independence, forming Republika Srpska (RS).

Although Slovenia, Croatia, and Bosnia were all admitted to the UN on May 22, 1992, for the next three and half years, violence raged across the region. This eventually came to an end in 1995. In Croatia, government forces launched a major military offensive that overran the RSK and brought its attempted secession to an end. In Bosnia, a massacre of over 8,000 Bosniaks carried out by Bosnian Serb forces in the town of Srebrenica galvanized international opinion and led to the NATO bombing campaign and eventually the signing of the Dayton

Peace Agreement. The Bosnian Serb entity was absorbed into the Bosnian state, albeit enjoying extensive autonomy.

Meanwhile, in the south of Yugoslavia another state had emerged. On September 8, 1991, Macedonia declared independence. Unlike the other republics, its independence was entirely peaceful. However, it was not entirely uncontested. It faced strong opposition from Greece, which argued that the new country was making irredentist claims on its northern province of Macedonia. Although it was eventually admitted to the UN on April 8, 1993, it did not join under its constitutional name, the Republic of Macedonia. Instead, it was admitted under a provisional designation—the Former Yugoslav Republic of Macedonia (FYROM). The dispute was eventually resolved in 2019, when the country changed its name to North Macedonia.

As a result of all this, what had been one country in 1990 had by 1995 become five independent states: Bosnia and Herzegovina, Croatia, Macedonia, Slovenia, and the Federal Republic of Yugoslavia (FRY), which was now made up of just two of the original republics, Montenegro and Serbia. Interestingly, though, only four of these states were UN members. In 1992, and in line with the findings of the Badinter Commission, the UN Security Council had decided that the SFRY had ceased to exist and that the FRY would have to apply for membership as a new state.[3] After refusing to do so for several years, the FRY eventually relented and was admitted to the UN on November 1, 2000. Importantly, while the Yugoslav conflict was bloody and violent, it in fact served to reinforce many of the key principles of secession and state creation that had been established since post-1945 decolonization.

3. UN Security Council Resolution 777, September 19, 1992.

Why did Czechoslovakia break apart peacefully?

The entirely peaceful breakup of countries tends to be rare. The most notable modern exception is the dissolution of Czechoslovakia. Taking place at the same time as the dissolutions of the Soviet Union and Yugoslavia, its breakup was also an outcome of the transition from a one-party, multinational federation to a free, multiparty political system. However, in marked contrast to the other cases, the dissolution of Czechoslovakia was entirely consensual, orderly, and completed without any violence.

Like Yugoslavia, Czechoslovakia was founded in 1918. In the decades that followed, there was a history of political and constitutional tensions between its two main peoples, Czechs and Slovaks. While in 1968 the country was transformed from a unitary state to a federation of two republics, the significance of this change was quite limited. As in the Soviet Union and Yugoslavia, the real government lay in the hands of the totalitarian Communist party. With the end of Communist rule in 1989, differences over the basic constitutional structure of the state emerged. Although public opinion polls had showed consistent opposition among both Czechs and Slovaks to the breakup of Czechoslovakia, in the June 1992 parliamentary elections, Czech voters supported parties that backed federal rule, whereas Slovaks supported parties that wanted a confederal system (nebulously defined as more than a federation but less than two independent states). Under these circumstances, no federal government could be formed. Fearing a paralyzing stalemate, the victorious political elites rejected a referendum on the breakup of the state. Instead, they opted for a legislative act of constitutional dissolution in the federal parliament. Eventually, the winning parties in the two republics agreed to establish a caretaker federal government that would terminate the federation and facilitate a smooth transition to independence for both republics. While regretted by many people in both republics, neither the rejection of a referendum nor the end of Czechoslovakia itself met with large-scale and active popular opposition. By the end of 1992 the Czech and Slovak Republics negotiated multiple treaties outlining their future relations and the two became independent on January 1, 1993. Both were promptly recognized by foreign states and both joined the UN on January 19, 1993.

How did the mergers that formed Germany and Yemen occur?

Although we tend to associate the end of the Cold War with the collapse and dissolution of countries, such as the Soviet Union and Yugoslavia, the first consequence of the fall of the Berlin Wall falling was in fact the merger of several states. First, there was the reunification of East and West Germany. This was followed by the unification of North and South Yemen. However, while these cases may appear similar, in truth they differ in important ways. Like Vietnam before it, and Korea to this day, Germany was a divided state. The split between East and West was understood to be temporary. Yemen, on the other hand, was a straightforward merger between two sovereign countries.

After the Second World War, the Allied Powers divided Germany into zones of control. In the west of the country, the United States, France, and Britain assumed control. In the east, the Soviet Union held sway. On May 23, 1949, the three zones in the west officially became the Federal Republic of Germany (FRG, West Germany). Months later, on October 7, 1949, the Soviet Zone became the German Democratic Republic (GDR, East Germany). From the outset, West Germany, which was admitted to the UN as an observer in 1955, refused to accept the independence of East Germany and claimed sovereignty over the entire German territory. By the early 1970s, relations between the two parts had improved. Although West Germany still refused to accept East Germany as an independent state, it agreed to normalize ties. In 1972, formal relations were established, and East Germany became a UN observer. On September 18, 1973, they were both admitted as full members of the UN.[4] In 1989, the communist government in East Germany fell, paving the way for democratic elections and negotiations to reunite the country. On October 3, 1990, the GDR ceased to exist. The provinces of East Germany were formally incorporated into the FRG, which continued to be internationally recognized and retained its seat at the UN.

Prior to their unification, North and South Yemen had very different histories. North Yemen, a part of the Ottoman Empire, achieved independence in 1918. In contrast, South Yemen, a British colony known as Aden, only became independent in 1967. Two years later, in 1969, the South fell under communist rule. This lasted until the 1980s when a combination of civil conflict and the end of the Cold War saw the two parts, which had maintained generally good relations, agree to unite. On May 22, 1990, the Arab Republic of Yemen (North Yemen) and the Socialist People's Republic of Yemen (South Yemen) ceased to exist, and an entirely new state was created, the Republic of Yemen. However, relations between the two parts of the new country soon deteriorated. In 1994, a civil war broke out and the South unilaterally declared independence. This went unrecognized by the international community and the government quickly reasserted its authority. Nevertheless, separatist sentiment remains strong in the South and an active independence campaign exists—the Southern Movement. In 2015, the country returned to civil war. Although not directly tied to the issue of secession, many in South Yemen hope that this will open the way to renewed statehood.

4. Usually countries are admitted singly—rather than as a group—to the UN. However, the East and West Germany were admitted under a single resolution, UN General Assembly Resolution 3050 (XXVIII), September 18, 1973. Interestingly, the Democratic People's Republic of Korea (North Korea) and the Republic of Korea (South Korea) were also admitted to the UN under one resolution, UN General Assembly Resolution 46/1, September 17, 1991.

Why is Somaliland unrecognized?

There is perhaps no better example of just how difficult it is for a territory to secede unilaterally and then gain international recognition than the case of Somaliland. Established in the late nineteenth century as British Somaliland—to distinguish it from Italian Somaliland, further to the south—the independent Republic of Somaliland gained independence on June 26, 1960, as part of the wider process of decolonization taking place at the time. Immediately recognized by more than thirty countries, including the United Kingdom, the republic existed for a mere matter of days. Following the independence of Italian Somaliland, on July 1, the two countries voluntarily united to form the Somali Republic. However, the union quickly soured. The next year, a new constitution downgraded Somaliland to an autonomous province of the Somali Republic, now known as the Federal Republic of Somalia. The jubilation that had greeted the creation of the union gave way to resentment as the region became increasingly marginalized over the following decades. When the south of the country disintegrated, Somaliland seized its chance to secede and reclaim its statehood. On May 18, 1991, it unilaterally declared independence.

To many observers, Somaliland appears to have a strong case for independence and recognition. It had already been a sovereign state, recognized by many countries—although, as noted in Chapter 1, this is not actually accepted as a justification for secession. It also meets the Montevideo criteria. Its boundaries are defined, and it has a settled population and effective governance—far more effective than Somalia. It has also established international contacts. It has representative offices in the United States and the United Kingdom, as well as in other European and African states. It has also received a considerable degree of international legitimization. Its officials often travel abroad and meet with political figures from other states. Moreover, in 2005, an AU fact-finding mission even noted that it amounted to a special case and should be recognized. However, while there is undoubtedly a great deal of sympathy for its case, this has not translated into formal acceptance of its statehood, even by its closest regional allies.

Again, this all goes to underscore just how reluctant countries are to recognize an act of secession against the will of the parent state—even when there are seemingly many good reasons for doing so.

How did Eritrea and South Sudan become independent?

The international community's opposition to secession meant that most separatist efforts since 1960 were either defeated or led to the creation of an unrecognized de facto state. Occasionally, though, a separatist campaign would be successful. After Bangladesh, perhaps the two best examples are Eritrea and South Sudan. The crucial difference is that while Bangladesh gained widespread recognition before it was accepted as independent by its parent state, these two cases—especially when considered alongside Somaliland—highlight that secession and recognition in the post-colonial world still remains largely dependent on the consent of the parent state.

Located in East Africa, Eritrea was conquered and colonized by Italy in 1889. In 1941, during the Second World War, the United Kingdom seized the territory. In November 1950, the UN General Assembly established a commission to determine the wishes of the people concerning their future. Based on its findings—which included a recognition of neighboring Ethiopia's historic claims to the territory and its need for access to the sea—the commission recommended that Eritrea should be an autonomous federal unit of Ethiopia.[5] On September 15, 1952, the Federation of Ethiopia and Eritrea was created, despite the wish of many Eritreans for their own independent state. In September 1961, an armed insurgency was launched. A year later, Ethiopia rescinded Eritrea's autonomy.

5. UN General Assembly Resolution 390 (V), December 2, 1950.

Over the next thirty years, the Eritrean People's Liberation Front (EPLF) and Ethiopia, supported by the Soviet Union, fought a bloody conflict. However, the end of the Cold War saw the end of Soviet assistance and the EPLF, which was now allied to a number of Ethiopian rebel groups, gained the military advantage. In May 1991, the EPLF and its allies entered Addis Ababa and the Ethiopian government fell. The new administration of Ethiopia now recognized the right of the Eritreans to vote on independence. In April 1993, a referendum showed that 99.8 percent supported statehood. On May 28, 1993, Eritrea joined the UN as its 182nd member.

Sudan was conquered by Ottoman Egypt in the nineteenth century, before coming under British colonial rule. However, there were always strong ethnic and religious differences between the northern and southern parts of the country. In 1956, when Sudan was granted independence, the south demanded autonomy. Although the Southern Sudan Autonomous Region was established in 1972, a decade later the Sudanese government revoked its self-rule and imposed Sharia law across the whole country. This led to the creation of the Sudan People's Liberation Army (SPLA). After many years of bitter fighting, the sides signed a peace agreement in 2005. The two parts of the country—with South Sudan having been a long-standing de facto state—agreed to share power and reached an agreement on sharing important mineral resources. Meanwhile, Sudanese troops would withdraw from the region. Most importantly, it was agreed that after six years a referendum would be held on the future of the territory. This was held January 9–15, 2011. Support for statehood was overwhelming (98.3 percent). Five months later, on July 14, 2011, South Sudan officially became an independent state. A week later it became the 193rd member of the UN. However, since then, the country has been wracked by fighting and is increasingly viewed as a failed state.

Have any secessions been put down by armed force since 1990?

Yes, although it is hard to pin down an exact figure. Again, it depends on what one considers to be a secessionist movement. That said, since the end of the Cold War several significant attempts at independence have been put down by armed force. Perhaps the three best known cases have been Russia's effort to retake control of Chechnya, Croatia's military operation to overrun the RSK, and Sri Lanka's defeat of the Tamil Tigers.

While the attempt by Bosnian Serbs to secede was eventually resolved when Republika Srpska was integrated into the Bosnian state, elsewhere in Yugoslavia another attempted secession was suppressed by armed force. As Croatia sought to break away from Yugoslavia, the country's Serbian community, representing 10–15 percent of the population, tried to secede from Croatia and remain in what was left of Yugoslavia. On December 19, 1991, they declared their own state, the RSK. Although Croatian forces attempted to fight back, the well-armed Serbs, supported by the Yugoslav army, resisted. In January 1992, a ceasefire came into force monitored by the UN. By that point, almost a quarter of the country lay beyond the control of the central government. More to the point, the main location of the RSK, at the center of the country, meant that Croatia was effectively cut in two. In late 1994, the international community launched a major effort to resolve the conflict. When this failed, the Croatian government prepared to retake the territory by force. On August 4, 1995, Croatia launched Operation Storm. In less than three days, Croat troops overran the RSK, forcing around 200,000 ethnic Serbs to flee. Today, Serbs make up less than 5 percent of the population.

One of the most violent secessionist campaigns of modern times was fought in a relatively small region of southern Russia. Approximately 6,900 square miles (17,200 square kilometers) in size, and with less than one and a half million inhabitants, the north Caucasus region of Chechnya was first incorporated into the Russian Empire in the late eighteenth century. While it enjoyed a brief period of independence in the early twentieth century, it was brought under Soviet control in 1921. As the Soviet Union broke up, Chechnya seized its opportunity to break away. In 1991, it unilaterally declared independence, forming the Chechen Republic of Ichkeria. As it had not been one of the federal republics of the Soviet Union, it was not considered eligible for statehood. Despite intensive lobbying, no country recognized it. At first, Moscow took relatively little notice of the attempted secession. However, as time passed, concern grew that it could become a model for other separatist regions. In 1994, Russian troops resorted to force. In the fierce fighting that followed, the capital city Grozny was all but flattened. But Russia was unable to reassert control over the mountainous territory. In 1996, a ceasefire was reached, and Russian forces withdrew. However, following continued secessionist activity, Moscow launched a new offensive in 1999. This time it put down the rebellion. Recognizing that it would not be able to maintain control through force of arms alone, Russia granted Chechnya considerable autonomy. While estimates from the two sides vary wildly, it is likely that around 100,000 died during the two wars.

The third major example occurred on the island of Sri Lanka, off the southern coast of India. A former British colony, following independence in 1948 tensions rose between the country's two main ethno-religious communities—the predominantly Buddhist Sinhalese, representing about 70 percent of the population, and the mostly Hindu Tamils, who made up 10 percent of the country's inhabitants. (The country also has large Muslim and Christian minorities.) By the 1970s, the country was increasingly wrecked by violence as the Tamils fought against Sinhalese rule. In 1976, Tamil militants formed the Liberation Tigers of Tamil Eelam (LTTE), more commonly known as the Tamil Tigers. Its objective was to establish a Tamil homeland in the northern tip of the country. In the years that followed, an increasingly violent civil war gripped the country as the LTTE managed to bring large parts of the east and north of the country under its control. Meanwhile, repeated attempts to reach a peaceful settlement to the conflict failed. In 2009, Sri Lankan armed forces defeated the LTTE and retook the north. However, it came at a high price. The UN has estimated that 80,000–100,000 people died during the conflict.

It is interesting to note that in all three cases there was subsequently widespread international criticism about the way in which the government and armed forces behaved, including accusations of war crimes and crimes against humanity. Some Croatian officials were even put on trial for their actions. However, in all three cases, the basic right of the parent state to retake their territories has never been fundamentally challenged by the international community.

Which other cases of secession could be put down by force?

Looking ahead, it is likely that we will see more attempted secessions quelled by armed force. High on the list of ongoing cases is Nagorno-Karabakh, a de facto state in the Caucasus. Inhabited predominantly by ethnic Armenians, it had been an autonomous area (*oblast*) of the Azerbaijan Soviet Socialist Republic. However, in 1988, it voted to unite with Armenia— a decision supported by the Armenian Supreme Soviet. In 1992, following the collapse of the Soviet Union, the Nagorno-Karabakh Republic (NKR) unilaterally declared independence. Although Azerbaijan managed to retake a large swathe of the province, the following year Armenian and Nagorno-Karabakh forces retook the land, as well as large tracts of Azeri territory before a ceasefire was reached. In 2007, Armenia and Azerbaijan were reported to have agreed on a set of basic principles governing a resolution to the conflict. These included the return of territories surrounding Nagorno-Karabakh to Azeri control, the creation of a corridor linking the territory to Armenia, and a "future determination of the final legal status of Nagorno-Karabakh through a legally binding expression of will."[6] To date, no state has recognized the NKR, and UN Security Council and General Assembly resolutions have been passed explicitly recognizing Azerbaijan's territorial integrity.[7] While peace talks have continued intermittently, there was a growing sense that Azerbaijan might be preparing to retake Nagorno-Karabakh by force. It used revenues from oil sales to buy weapons. Indeed, in some years, the Azerbaijani expenditure on defense is greater than the entire Armenian state budget. There were mounting tensions and repeated armed skirmishes along the ceasefire line with serious clashes taking place in 2016 and summer 2020.

The most serious armed engagement since the early 1990s took place in the fall of 2020 during which Azerbaijan recovered all the Armenian-held territories around Nagorno-Karabakh and a slice of the territory itself. Although the subsequent arrival of Russian peacekeepers makes a resumption of major fighting unlikely, their future withdrawal (they are to stay for five years with either party having the option of requesting their departure at that time) may well lead to a renewed campaign by Azerbaijan to regain control of the whole of the territory.

6. "Joint Statement on the Nagorno-Karabakh Conflict by U.S. President Obama, Russian President Medvedev, and French President Sarkozy at the L'Aquila Summit of the Eight, July 10, 2009," White House, July 10, 2009.
7. See, for example, "General Assembly Adopts Resolution Reaffirming Territorial Integrity of Azerbaijan, Demanding Withdrawal of All Armenian Forces," United Nations Department of Public Information, March 14, 2008. The vote passed 37–7, with 100 abstentions. The seven countries that opposed the resolution were: Angola, Armenia, France, India, Russian Federation, the United States, and Vanuatu.

Are any secessionist disputes resolved peacefully without independence?

Yes. Although many recent secessionist efforts have been put down by armed force, occasionally a separatist conflict will be resolved by a peaceful negotiation process. One of the most successful examples of this in recent times was the 2005 agreement between Aceh and Indonesia.

Located at the northwestern end of the Indonesian archipelago, the energy-rich province of Aceh is home to approximately four million people. Having always regarded itself as different from the rest of Indonesia, not least of all because it tended to be more conservatively Islamic than the rest of the country, discontent began to grow in the 1960s. In December 1976, the Free Aceh Movement (GAM) launched an armed uprising to end Indonesian rule and establish an independent state. Indonesia responded with a counter-insurgency campaign.

Having secured major victories against GAM, by the end of the decade it looked as if the attempt at secession was over. However, at the end of the 1980s, GAM resurfaced and fighting resumed. In 1999, after two decades of conflict, the first formal peace talks were brokered between the sides. These lasted until 2003, when they broke down and the Indonesian government began an all-out offensive to end the insurgency. Ultimately, though, it was a natural disaster that played the decisive role in ending the conflict. On December 26, 2004, a massive earthquake struck just off the coast off Aceh, followed by a devastating tsunami. Under these circumstances the armed quest for independence was unsustainable. A new peace initiative was launched under the auspices of Martti Ahtisaari, former president of Finland. Eight months later, on August 15, 2005, the government of Indonesia and GAM signed a peace agreement that brought the conflict to a close with Aceh remaining in Indonesia.[8]

8. "Memorandum of Understanding between the Government of the Republic of Indonesia and the Free Aceh Movement," August 15, 2005.

Why did Montenegro join the UN, but not Kosovo?

One of the clearest illustrations of the difficult position faced by territories seeking independence against the will of a parent state can be seen by comparing the cases of Montenegro and Kosovo. As noted earlier, by the end of 1995, the breakup of Yugoslavia led to the emergence of five new states. However, two more countries were still to follow: Montenegro and Kosovo. And yet, while Montenegro gained immediate recognition from the international community, Kosovo is still struggling to gain full international acceptance.

As noted, Montenegro was one of the six republics that made up the SFRY. However, unlike the other republics it decided to remain with Serbia as the federation collapsed. This was largely due to the fact that traditionally Serbia and Montenegro enjoyed very close relations. Many Montenegrins identify as Serbian, and many Serbs have Montenegrin ancestry. However, during the wars of the 1990s, relations between the two republics became strained, and by the end of the decade Montenegro began pressing for independence as well.

To prevent further fragmentation in the region, the European Union brokered an agreement to keep the two states united within a looser political arrangement. On February 4, 2003, the Federal Republic of Yugoslavia ceased to exist and was replaced by the State Union of Serbia and Montenegro. However, under the terms of the Constitutional Charter that formed the State Union,[9] it was agreed that the two parts would have the chance to break away after three years. As this date approached, Montenegro announced that it intended to hold an independence referendum. On May 21, 2006, voters decided by 55.5 percent to secede. Two weeks later, on June 4, the parliament of Montenegro formally declared independence.

9. "Constitutional Charter of the State Union of Serbia and Montenegro," Adopted in Belgrade, January 27, 2003, http://www.worldstatesmen. org/SerbMont_Const_2003.pdf.

As the process had been accepted by Serbia, Montenegro was quickly recognized by the international community. On June 28, 2006, it became the 192nd member of the UN. Meanwhile, on June 3, the Republic of Serbia had informed the UN Secretary-General that it would continue the UN membership held by the State Union.

In contrast to Montenegro, Kosovo was never a republic within Yugoslavia. Instead, it was an autonomous province of Serbia—albeit one that had a seat on the Yugoslav federal executive council alongside the republics. In 1989, its self-rule was abolished. As Yugoslavia collapsed, the province's majority ethnic Albanian population organized an unofficial referendum on statehood and unilaterally declared independence on September 22, 1991. However, this was recognized only by neighboring Albania. The international community refused to recognize it. Under the terms of the Badinter Commission, which had been formed to look into the dissolution of Yugoslavia, Kosovo, as a sub-state unit of Serbia, was not regarded as having the right to independence alongside the six republics.

In the mid-1990s, an armed uprising was launched against Serb rule, and by 1999 this had brought the province to the verge of civil war. Following a failed peace process, NATO launched a military campaign against Serbia with the result that, after seventy-eight days of aerial bombing, the Serbian government sued for peace. Under the terms of UN Security Council Resolution 1244, Yugoslavia's sovereignty over Kosovo was reaffirmed. However, the province was placed under UN administration pending a final decision on its status. In 2006, a negotiation process began under UN auspices. (Interestingly, this process was also led by Martti Ahtisaari, who had just resolved the Aceh dispute discussed in the previous question.) While Serbia was willing to offer extensive autonomy, the Kosovo Albanians demanded independence. Meanwhile, hopes of reaching an agreement in the Security Council were also blocked. Russia, which supported

Serbia, argued that only a mutually agreeable solution would be acceptable. In contrast, the United States, United Kingdom, and France were worried that a failure to give Kosovo independence would lead to regional instability. With no prospect of an agreement, on February 17, 2008, Kosovo unilaterally declared independence.

The decision to declare independence led to deep divisions within the international community. On the one side were those states—such as Russia and China, as well as regional powers, such as India, Brazil, and South Africa—that took the view that it amounted to an unauthorized act of secession without Serbia's consent and should not be recognized. On the other hand, the United States and many Western states—such as the United Kingdom, France, and Germany—argued that Kosovo was a unique case (sui generis) in international politics due to the history of human rights abuses committed by Serbia, the period spent under UN administration, and the special status Kosovo held in Yugoslavia. Although it was not a republic, it did enjoy many rights equivalent to one. They therefore argued that its independence should not be regarded as an ordinary case of unilateral secession. Even today, international opinion remains remarkably evenly divided on the issues. As of late 2021, 98 of the UN's 193 members recognize Kosovo as an independent state, whereas 95 do not. (The number had been higher, reaching 113 at one point, but Serbia managed to persuade around 15 countries to rescind their recognition.) However, any hope of joining the UN, and thus gaining full admission into the international community, looks poor. Neither Russia nor China, which retain a veto over UN membership, show any intention of changing their position on Kosovo.

The difference between Montenegro and Kosovo casts a valuable light on secession in international politics. Ultimately, the crucial difference between them is that Montenegro, although far smaller than Kosovo in terms of population, was a republic and thus deemed to have a right to independence under the terms of the Badinter Commission, whereas Kosovo, which had in many ways enjoyed the rights of a republic, was officially classed as a province of Serbia and so did not enjoy the right to statehood. This vital constitutional and theoretical difference, though very small in real terms in Yugoslavia, made a world of difference in terms of how the two came to be treated by the international community. Whereas Montenegro's independence was seen as the product of the dissolution of Yugoslavia, Kosovo's independence came to be regarded as a case of unilateral secession.

What did the International Court of Justice say about Kosovo's UDI?

One of the most interesting aspects of Kosovo's secession was the decision by the UN General Assembly, acting on Serbia's initiative, to ask the International Court of Justice for an advisory opinion on whether Kosovo's declaration of independence was in accordance with international law. This became the most important case ever put before the court, the world's highest authority on matters relating to international law, on the question of secession. Indeed, it is the only case in the court's history where all five permanent members of the Security Council also took part in the proceedings.

In July 2010, the court delivered an opinion. In a landmark decision, it argued that, except where specifically prohibited, such as by a Security Council resolution, general international law contained no prohibitions of unilateral declarations of independence. Moreover, having considered the specific circumstances in Kosovo's case, it ruled that there was no reason to argue that its declaration of independence had violated international law. In essence, the court argued that declarations of independence should be seen as mere statements. Anyone can declare independence. Effectively, it is whether that declaration of independence is recognized and accepted that really matters. Crucially, and contrary to what many seem to think, the court was also adamant that its decision took absolutely no position on whether Kosovo was a state. Nor did it consider whether states that had recognized Kosovo had violated the UN Charter's requirement for members to respect the territorial integrity of one another. As it said, it was not asked to address either of these questions and so it avoided doing so.[10]

Will Abkhazia and South Ossetia gain wider acceptance?

Just months after Kosovo's declaration of independence, international attention became focused on another couple of highly controversial and interrelated cases of secession: Abkhazia and South Ossetia.

Although both had been a part of Georgia during the Soviet era, they declared independence following the breakup of the USSR. While actively supporting them by the mid-2000s, Moscow had nevertheless held back from formally recognizing them. This changed after Kosovo's declaration of independence. Aggrieved at what it felt were Western double standards, Moscow shifted its stance. Following growing tensions along the South Ossetia–Georgian boundary, war broke out between Russia and Georgia on August 7, 2008. Three weeks later, after having defeated Georgia, Moscow announced that it had recognized the two entities as independent states. Although the decision was strongly condemned by many countries, including the United States, United Kingdom, and France, Russia's place on the Security Council meant that it was impossible to pass a UN resolution condemning the decision. Meanwhile, Moscow lobbied other states for recognition. Within weeks, Venezuela and Nicaragua, as well as the Pacific

10. International Court of Justice, "Accordance with international law of the unilateral declaration of independence in respect of Kosovo (Request for Advisory Opinion)," July 22, 2010. See also Marko Milanovic and Michael Wood (editors), *The Law and Politics of the Kosovo Advisory Opinion* (Oxford: Oxford University Press, 2015).

island states of Nauru, Tuvalu, and Vanuatu, all announced that they had recognized Abkhazia and South Ossetia. Then, in 2018, they were recognized by Syria. However, no other UN members followed suit. Even some of Russia's closest allies, such as Belarus, have refused to recognize them.

As things stand, it seems extremely unlikely that either territory will gain wider recognition. For a start, few believe that South Ossetia is a viable state. Its future would therefore seem to be either an agreed reintegration back into Georgia or, more likely, annexation by Russia. After Crimea, this seems less far-fetched than it once was. On the other hand, Abkhazia is generally accepted as a de facto state. While it too may be reincorporated back into Georgia, most probably with a very high degree of autonomy, or annexed by Russia, it may yet be able to carve out a place for itself and one day be accepted as an independent country. However, this seems to be unlikely for the foreseeable future. The Georgian government continues to assert its sovereignty over both territories and is supported by the United States and the European Union.

Why did Crimea declare independence before being annexed by Russia?

One of the most unusual acts of secession in recent years was the declaration of independence by the short-lived Republic of Crimea just two days before it was incorporated into Russia. While it may have seemed odd that a territory that was about to be claimed by another state would declare independence, the decision can in fact be readily explained in the context of international law and as an attempt to add a veneer of legality to what was otherwise a violation of the territorial integrity of a UN member.

Historically, the Crimean Peninsula had been a part of Russia. However, in 1954, it was transferred to Ukraine. Crucially, when the USSR dissolved, Russia affirmed Ukraine's sovereignty over the autonomous territory. However, it insisted that

Ukraine sign a lease permitting the continued stationing of the Russian Black Sea naval fleet in the peninsula. In February 2014, following the overthrow of a pro-Russian government in Ukraine, Moscow sent troops into the Crimea and installed a puppet regime. On March 6, the Crimean Parliament called a referendum on whether to remain a part of Ukraine, albeit under an obsolete constitutional structure, or join Russia. Despite strong condemnation from the international community, the vote went ahead ten days later, and 97 percent voted to unite with Russia. The next day, the Crimean Parliament formally declared independence and issued an appeal to join the Russian Federation. Russia promptly recognized the Republic of Crimea as an independent state. The Russian Parliament ratified the Treaty of Accession of the Republic of Crimea just days later.

The unilateral declaration of independence was clearly never meant to lead to the creation of a sovereign state. It was merely a device to facilitate Russia's absorption of the peninsula. This could not have happened if Crimea was still a part of Ukraine as a direct annexation would be a conspicuous violation of Ukraine's territorial integrity. However, if Crimea declared independence, and this was recognized by Russia, the fiction could then be created that Crimea's union with Russia was an act of self-determination by a sovereign state. As Russia is a permanent member of the Security Council, it was not possible to pass a resolution condemning either Crimea's declaration of independence or Russia's forcible incorporation of the peninsula. However, the UN General Assembly reaffirmed the sovereignty and territorial integrity of Ukraine and called on states and international organizations not to recognize any claimed alteration of Crimea's status.[11]

---

11. UN General Assembly Resolution 68/262, March 27, 2014.

Have Canada and the United Kingdom created a democratic model of secession?

Although almost all states have actively opposed secession, often violently, there have been rare examples of states that have opened the way for parts of their territory to gain independence. Both Canada and the United Kingdom have attempted to deal with secession in a consensual and peaceful manner. In their separate ways, they have helped to clarify how a lawful and democratic process of secession can be created. However, as can also be seen, even if a state is willing to allow secession at one point, it does not hold that it will be open to the idea at a later stage.

In 1763, Quebec was ceded to Great Britain by France. As a British territory and then a province of Canada, Quebec has retained a French-language identity. In 1977, the province elected an administration promising a sovereignty-association that would see Quebec become independent in most regards but would allow it to share certain functions with Canada, such as a currency. Although this plan was defeated in a referendum (59.6–40.5 percent) in May 1980, calls for change continued. In 1995, another vote was held, this time on full independence. It was defeated by the narrowest of margins—50.6–49.2 percent. Following this, the Canadian government asked the country's Supreme Court for an opinion as to whether Quebec could potentially secede unilaterally. It asked three questions: did the Canadian constitution give the political institutions of Quebec the ability to pursue a unilateral act of secession? Did international law give those institutions the right to secede unilaterally? And, finally, in the event of a clash between Canadian law and international law, which would take precedence? In response, the court argued that there was no right to unilateral secession under either Canadian law or international law, and thus, there was no clash between the two. However, in the event Quebec clearly voted to secede, Canada should negotiate separation.[12] Based on this, the Canadian Parliament passed the Clarity Act, in June 2000.[13] This sets out the way in which secession should be handled. First, any referendum question must be clear. Second, in the event of a vote for statehood, any subsequent negotiations must be held with all the provinces of Canada, as well as the country's indigenous peoples. Third, any act of secession would require an amendment to the Canadian Constitution—thereby curtailing the possibility of unilateral secession. Crucially, though, neither the Supreme Court ruling, nor the ensuing Clarity Act, have been accepted by the Quebec government. Canada therefore remains a country that, while accepting a possibility of secession, does not have an agreed-upon procedure for carrying it out.

For many centuries, Scotland existed as an independent kingdom. However, in 1707, following a decision by their respective parliaments, Scotland and England formally united into a single state. In 2011, the Scottish National Party (SNP) was elected to government in Scotland. As the SNP had openly campaigned for an independence vote, the British government saw no choice but to allow a referendum on statehood. On October 15, 2012, the British government and the Scottish government settled on the terms of the vote. It would have to have a clear legal base; be legislated for by the Scottish Parliament; be conducted to command the confidence of parliaments, governments, and people; and deliver a fair test and a decisive expression of the views of people in Scotland and a result that everyone will respect.[14] Almost two years later, on September

12. Supreme Court of Canada, "Reference re Secession of Quebec," August 20, 1998.
13. An Act to give effect to the requirement for clarity as set out in the opinion of the Supreme Court of Canada in the Quebec Secession, July 29, 2000.
14. "Agreement between the United Kingdom Government and the Scottish Government on a referendum on independence for Scotland," Edinburgh, October 15, 2012.

18, 2014, Scottish voters decided by 55–45 percent to reject independence. While the British government claimed at the time that the vote had settled the matter for the foreseeable future, the SNP insisted that another vote could be held again if a significant change in circumstances occurs. The decision of the United Kingdom to leave the European Union, which was rejected by Scottish voters, is widely seen in Scotland as grounds for such a vote. In March 2017, the Scottish Parliament passed a motion opening the way for discussions on another referendum.[15] However, in contrast to the position taken earlier, the British government now stands against a new referendum on independence. Arguing that the referendum had been billed as a "once in a generation" vote, it also argues that the United Kingdom needs stability following its departure from the European Union. Undeterred, the Scottish government under the SNP has insisted that it is still intent on pressing ahead with a vote. This raises the very real prospect of a constitutional showdown over the issue.

Aside from the democratic way in which Canada and the United Kingdom responded to independence movements in Quebec and Scotland, the two examples are instructive in a couple of other ways. Firstly, they show that secessionism is ubiquitous. It is not a problem confined to poor and politically oppressed regions. Even wealthy and well-functioning liberal democracies can have powerful separatist movements. Secondly, and perhaps even more significantly, both cases have shown that, if given a free choice, people will not always vote to secede. All this said, at a more general level, it is also worth noting that their democratic approach to secession has so far had very little wider impact. Few other countries appear willing to follow their lead.

---

15. "Scottish parliament votes for second independence referendum," *The Guardian*, March 28, 2017.

Why did Catalonia and Kurdistan fail to achieve independence?

Fall 2017 was a fascinating time for anyone interested in secession and state creation as both the Iraqi region of Kurdistan and the Spanish province of Catalonia held independence referendums within a week of each other. And yet, within a couple of months of these votes, both their prospects for statehood had all but disappeared for the foreseeable future.

Of all the peoples vying for independence, it has often been said that the Kurds are the largest ethnic group in the world without their own state. Predominantly Sunni Muslim and speaking an Indo-European language, the Kurds had been granted a right to choose an independent state at the end of the First World War under the terms of the Treaty of Sevres. However, their state never materialized. The creation of the Republic of Turkey, which covered much of the area that would have been ceded to the Kurds, put an end to the plan. Instead, the Kurds now found themselves scattered across Turkey, Iran, Iraq, Syria, and Soviet Armenia. The quest for statehood returned to international attention when the Kurdistan Workers Party (PKK) launched an armed campaign to establish a Kurdish state in the southeastern provinces of Turkey.

Although the conflict in Turkey continues, the most likely prospect for a Kurdish state instead came to lie with the Kurdish community in neighboring Iraq. Following the end of the First Gulf War, in 1991, they gained considerable autonomy, eventually becoming a federal region in 2005. Thereafter, Iraqi Kurdistan essentially became a de facto state. In the years that followed, calls for independence grew. Despite opposition from much of the international community, the Kurdistan Regional Government (KRG) eventually held a referendum on statehood on September 25, 2017. Although the results showed 93 percent support for statehood on a 73 percent turnout, the vote was immediately rejected by the Iraqi government, key international actors, including

the United States,[16] and powerful regional neighbors, such as
Iran and Turkey. Under these circumstances, a declaration of
independence had no chance of success. Following clashes
between Iraqi and Kurdish forces, which saw large swathes
of territory in northern Iraq claimed by Iraqi Kurdistan come
back under the control of the Iraqi central government, the result of the referendum was "frozen" and the president of the
KRG resigned. Meanwhile, the Iraqi government announced
that after years of tolerating the region's extensive autonomy,
it would now seek to extend its control over the territory. As
a result, the prospects of a Kurdish state now emerging seem
as dim as ever.

At the same time, Catalonia's attempt to break away also
met with an ignominious end. Situated in the northeast of the
Iberian Peninsula, Catalonia is the sixth largest and second most
populous of Spain's nineteen provinces. It is also the country's
wealthiest. In 2014, following several years of growing pro-
independence sentiment, the Catalan government announced
that it intended to hold a referendum. However, the plan was
cancelled after Spain's Constitutional Court ruled that the
vote would be unconstitutional, and the Spanish government
announced that it would take all necessary steps to prevent
it from taking place. Instead, Catalan authorities organized
a non-binding, unofficial poll. This indicated 80 percent support for independence on a turnout of 40 percent. In regional
elections the following year, pro-independence parties managed to win a majority in the regional assembly and called a
referendum on October 1, 2017.

Despite strong efforts by Spanish police to prevent the
vote, the result showed 92 percent support for independence on a turnout of 43 percent. Days after the vote, the
Catalan Parliament passed a declaration of independence, but

16. "Tillerson says Kurdish independence referendum is illegitimate,
Washington Post, September 29, 2017.

immediately suspended it pending talks with the Spanish government. However, Madrid refused to negotiate. As a result, the Catalan Parliament unilaterally declared independence on October 27, 2017. The announcement was immediately rejected by numerous countries, including the United States, United Kingdom, and France. Meanwhile, Spain responded by imposing direct rule over Catalonia pending new regional elections. As several members of the Catalan administration were arrested on charges of rebellion, the Catalan president fled the province and announced the formation of a government in exile in Belgium. While the quest for an independent Catalonia is likely to continue, the immediate hopes of an independent Republic of Catalonia came to an end.

In their separate ways, the failed attempts by leaders in Kurdistan and Catalonia to secure independence once again underlines just how difficult it is for territories to secede unilaterally in the present era. While there was undoubtedly considerable international sympathy for both causes, their efforts to secure statehood without prior permission from their parent states forced the international community to fall back on their long-standing opposition to unauthorized efforts to break away. Nevertheless, the sheer speed by which their efforts to break away collapsed after they went ahead with their referendums came as a surprise to many observers and will almost certainly be studied in detail by other secessionist movements.

Is Taiwan a case of secession?

Taiwan is an important and fascinating case in any discussion on statehood in the modern world. However, and contrary to widespread belief, Taiwan is not actually a case of secession—although it could become one in the future. Instead, it is a rather unusual case in international politics. Formally, it is in fact a dispute over the recognition of a government, rather than a question of state recognition.

In the 1940s, China was ravaged by a civil war between the Nationalist government of the Republic of China and Communist Party forces led by Mao Tse-tung. By the end of the decade, the Nationalists were losing heavily. They fled the mainland and set up their base on the island of Taiwan, off the east coast of mainland China. Despite having lost control of the mainland, the Nationalists continued to claim to be the legitimate government of the entire country. With the support of the West, they continued to occupy the country's seat at the UN. However, by the late 1960s, the tide was turning. An increasing number of states were recognizing the Communist-led PRC. On October 25, 1971, the UN General Assembly passed Resolution 2758 expelling the representatives of the Republic of China and recognizing the government of the PRC as the legitimate representative of China to the UN.

In the years that followed, more states switched their recognition, including the United States, in 1979. Today, around a dozen UN members and the Vatican continue to recognize Taiwan, as the Republic of China is generally known, as the legitimate government of China.[17] Although it no longer enjoys official recognition, Taiwan maintains extensive unofficial contacts with many countries, including the United States and many EU members. It is also still represented in many international bodies, including some specialized UN agencies—albeit under the designation Taiwan Province of China—and competes in the Olympic Games as Chinese Taipei.

Importantly, Taiwan has never formally sought independence. The constitutional position of both Taiwan and the PRC is that there is only one China. However, there is an independence movement in the island. In response, Beijing has frequently said that it would oppose any attempt by Taiwan

---

17. As of early 2022, the UN members still recognizing the Republic of China were Belize, Guatemala, Haiti, Honduras, Marshall Islands, Nauru, Palau, Paraguay, Saint Kitts and Nevis, Saint Lucia, Saint Vincent and the Grenadines, Eswatini, and Tuvalu.

to declare independence, even using military means. Under Article 8 of the Anti-Secession Law, which came into force on March 14, 2005, the Chinese parliament has authorized the government to take "non-peaceful" steps if Taiwan attempted to secede.

Why is Palestine not a UN member?

The status of Palestine is one of the world's most enduring and controversial examples of contested statehood. Although the issue predates the process leading to the end of the European colonial empires, it has come to be treated as an instance of unfinished decolonization. The problem is that while there is universal agreement that the Palestinians have a right to a state, there has been no agreement between the Israelis and Palestinians on the borders, population, capital, and other elements of an independent Palestine.

Following the Second World War, the United Kingdom decided to withdraw from Palestine, which it had governed since the First World War. In 1947, the UN General Assembly recommended the creation of two states in the territory, one Arab and the other Jewish. The Palestinian Arabs rejected the UN partition plan and, in May 1948, joined neighboring Arab states in an unsuccessful attack against the newly declared State of Israel. As a result, the Jewish state cemented its existence. However, no Palestinian state was formed. In 1967, Israel defeated another attack by its neighbors and occupied the entire territory of Palestine, including East Jerusalem, the West Bank, and Gaza. In 1988, Palestinian leaders in exile declared the creation of the State of Palestine. This received limited recognition. In 1993, under the terms of the Oslo Accords, a Palestinian Authority was created as a precursor to a final settlement based on the eventual creation of a Palestinian state.

At present, the situation on the ground is in limbo. The Palestinian Authority, presenting itself as the government of the revived State of Palestine, controls little more than parts of the West Bank. Despite this, it now enjoys widespread recognition, and most UN members have established diplomatic relations with it. In 2011, it applied to join the UN. However, the recommendation needed to allow it to go to a final vote in the General Assembly was blocked by the United States. Nevertheless, in 2012, 138 UN members voted to make it a "non-member observer state" of the UN. It also became a "state party" to the Rome Statute establishing the International Criminal Court and was admitted as a full member of UNESCO. However, Israel, the United States, and many European countries refuse to accept it as a state. They argue that a Palestinian state can only be established in a comprehensive peace agreement with Israel. US opposition means that Palestine will not get the necessary approval required for full UN membership for the foreseeable future without a political settlement.

Was the Islamic State a genuine state?

No. Despite its name and a superficial resemblance to a state—a governing structure that controls a territory and inhabitants across Syria and Iraq—the so-called Islamic State—otherwise known as ISIS or IS—was not a state. For the last 400 years, a claim of statehood has presupposed that there are other states in relation to which one is sovereign and independent. A state's territory and population have necessarily required boundaries. However, the Islamic State did not accept the idea of boundaries or state sovereignty. Regarding itself as the true representative of the only valid religion and political philosophy, the Islamic State believed itself the only legitimate territorial entity. It did not ask foreign states for recognition; it in fact wanted to overturn the system of multiple states. This, along with terrorism and extreme violence, generated nearly universal opposition to the Islamic State, which virtually guaranteed its demise. The example of the Islamic State shows that a state is not simply a sum of physical components.

Statehood requires not only governance of a territory and population but also international legitimacy.

Will any more states emerge from decolonization?

While it is possible that new states will emerge in future through secession, dissolution, or merger, it is unlikely that many more will be created by decolonization. The heyday of decolonization was between 1950 and 1980, when the number of UN members rose from 60 to 154. The large majority of these new states emerged as the old European empires withdrew from Africa, Asia, the South Pacific, and the Caribbean. In contrast, over the past three decades less than half of the twenty-nine new members of the UN have been the product of direct decolonization.

According to the UN, there are now just seventeen Non-Self-Governing Territories (NSGTs) around the world that have yet to be decolonized, though in several cases this classification is disputed by administering powers. These include one territory in Africa (Western Sahara); one in Europe (Gibraltar); six in the Pacific (American Samoa, French Polynesia, Guam, New Caledonia, Pitcairn, and Tokelau); and nine in the Atlantic and the Caribbean (Anguilla, Bermuda, British Virgin Islands, Cayman Islands, Falkland Islands, Montserrat, St. Helena, Turks and Caicos Islands, and the US Virgin Islands). Each is very small. Indeed, taken together, these territories amount to fewer than two million people.

While it is certainly possible that some of these territories may wish to become independent at some point, this does not mean that we should expect to see seventeen new states. Many of the remaining colonial remnants seem to have little desire for statehood. They prefer to maintain some form of relationship with the colonial authority. In other cases, independence is unlikely for practical, legal, or political reasons. Under the terms of the 1713 Treaty of Utrecht, the tiny territory of Gibraltar, which lies at the southern tip of the Iberian

Peninsula, was ceded to the United Kingdom in perpetuity. If the United Kingdom were to relinquish control, Gibraltar would be returned to Spain. Moreover, the people of the territory have insisted that they wish to remain under British rule. In a referendum on the issue, held in 2002 without the formal consent of the British government, they voted overwhelmingly (98.9 percent) to reject a proposal for shared British-Spanish sovereignty. Since then, the British government, which insists Gibraltar is self-governing, has said that it will "never" enter into discussion over the future of the territory without the agreement of the government of Gibraltar and its inhabitants. The Falkland Islands, which originally became a British Crown Colony in 1840, and is today a self-governing British Overseas Territory, is claimed by Argentina (which calls them the Malvinas). Again, the inhabitants have asserted their wish to remain under British rule. In a referendum held in 2013, 99.8 percent (on a 92 percent turnout) voted in favor of remaining a British Overseas Territory.

Conceivably, though perhaps controversially, one could expand the list to include other territories. For example, France maintains some overseas departments, such as Réunion, in the Indian Ocean, or Martinique, in the Caribbean. While originally colonial holdings, they are now regarded as integral parts of the French state. They have seats in the French Parliament and are fully part of the European Union. More correctly, therefore, any attempt by these territories to break away would be officially classed by France as secession. But it is rather academic. Of these, the most likely candidate for independence is the French territory of New Caledonia. However, it rejected independence in three referendums held in 2018, 2020, and 2021. As for the others, there seems little desire for statehood. In referendums held in French Guiana and Martinique, in 2010, inhabitants voted by 70 and 80 percent respectively against more autonomy, let alone full independence. Nevertheless, one could perhaps envisage the possibility, even if rather remote, that these territories may wish to pursue full independence at some point in the future.

Which country will be the next UN member state?

It is extremely hard to say. There are many peoples around the world vying for independence. However, ten or so territories stand out as the most likely candidates. Leading the pack are three South Pacific territories. The first is Bougainville—a mineral-rich island off the east coast of Papua New Guinea. Once administered by Australia, it was decolonized as a part of Papua New Guinea in 1975. However, this was resisted locally and a bloody conflict broke out. In 2001, a peace agreement was signed granting autonomy to the province and providing for a referendum on its future status—including the option of independence—within 10–15 years.[18] In December 2019, it voted overwhelmingly in favor of independence. However, while the government of Papua New Guinea has accepted the result, there are fears that it may yet decide not to honor it. The second is the French colony of New Caledonia, noted earlier. A third possibility is Chuuk. One of the four units of the Federated States of Micronesia, it has been planning to hold a vote on independence for several years. However, this has been postponed on several occasions for reasons that are not entirely clear.

Beyond this, the best candidates would seem to be some of the cases explored in this chapter. A strong contender would be Somaliland, which has a high degree of international acceptance already. Many observers suspect that if one major African country recognized it, others would follow. Next come Palestine and Kosovo. However, they are presently unable to obtain the necessary recommendations from the Security

---

18. "Bougainville Peace Agreement," August 30, 2001, http://peacema
ker.un.org/png-bougainville-agreement2001.

Council. (This will be explored in more detail in Chapter 6.) In the case of Palestine, the United States has made it clear that it would veto any attempt at membership in the absence of a peace agreement between Israel and Palestine. Kosovo faces a block by Russia and China.

Then there is always the possibility that another independence referendum could be held in Quebec or Scotland. Of the two, Scotland seems to be the more likely to have another go at securing independence within the next few years. Indeed, prominent leaders of the SNP insist that another vote is "inevitable." Less likely, but another possible contender for statehood, is Western Sahara. As noted, Kurdistan and Catalonia, once potentially strong contenders, have recently dropped down the list of possible new states. Their attempts to force the issue of independence appear to have backfired. Another possible contender is Greenland, which would secede from Denmark. However, while there has been talk of independence over the years, it seems unlikely that a vote will be held in the immediate future.

Finally, there is also the chance that we could see the dissolution of several federations and the emergence of several new countries. Interestingly, the most obvious candidates at present are the two most populous countries in Africa: Nigeria and Ethiopia. Both have seen growing inter-ethnic tensions. In Ethiopia, a bitter civil war has erupted in the northern province of Tigray. This has also fed separatist violence in Oromia, the largest of the country's federal provinces, and elsewhere. In Nigeria, there have been growing tensions in several states, including those that compose the former territory of Biafra, and between the predominantly Muslim north and the largely Christian south.

While these would seem to be the best candidates to be the next members of the UN, it may be the case that the next member is not on this list. There may well be some surprises on the horizon.

5

INDEPENDENCE AND THE INSTITUTIONS OF STATEHOOD

How are new states created?

The history of state creation over the past two and a half centuries shows that there are essentially six main ways in which a new state can come into existence. Two of these, original acquisition and gradual devolution, belong to the past. Original acquisition occurred through outside settlement of a territory belonging to no recognized state and the subsequent establishment of a state on that territory. The best-known example is Liberia, which was founded by African American settlers in 1847. The other historical method is gradual devolution, by which a government gradually devolved its powers to its overseas settler territory to the point that the constitutional links between the two were extinguished. Australia, New Zealand, and Canada became states through gradual devolution from the United Kingdom in the twentieth century. Since there remain no unsettled territories and no obvious overseas settler territories wishing to acquire attributes of statehood, we are unlikely to see new states established through these two methods.

In the modern era, the two most common forms of state creation have been decolonization and secession. The emergence of new states through decolonization has now all but stopped. However, as will be seen a little later, there are still some new states that could yet emerge via this route. In contrast, it seems highly likely that most of the new states of the twenty-first century will be created through secession. The most recent member of the UN, South Sudan, is the product of secession.

Finally, there are two more methods by which states can come into existence. The first is dissolution. This occurs when an existing state collapses into several separate and independent parts. The most obvious examples of this were Czechoslovakia and the Soviet Union. At present, it is hard to say whether we will see any further cases of dissolution in the foreseeable future. The other method of state creation is through merger. As we have seen, this happened in the case of Germany and Yemen. However, other examples included the short-lived United Arab Republic (UAR), which emerged following the decision of Egypt and Syria to unite, in 1958, and Tanzania, which was created in 1964 following the merger between Tanganyika and Zanzibar (both of which had joined the UN in 1961). Looking ahead, a merger could one day take place between North and South Korea. Also, we could potentially see a union between Kosovo and Albania. Although both officially deny that this is their policy, political figures in both countries have raised it as a possibility. Unification between Romania and Moldova is another possibility and there is also a long-standing agreement in principle for a union between Russia and Belarus.

How does secession differ from dissolution and decolonization?

Although they all share similar outcomes in terms of the creation of new states, secession, dissolution, and decolonization need to be distinguished from one another. The main difference between secession and dissolution is that in the aftermath of secession the parent state continues to exist as an independent and sovereign entity on the world stage. In the case of dissolution, the parent state ceases to exist. Interestingly, many cases of state dissolution have in fact started out as a process of secession by a constituent unit, but then the process spun out of control. This was seen in the case of the collapse of the Soviet Union, which began with an attempt by the Baltic republics to reassert their sovereignty, and the disintegration of Yugoslavia, which started with the attempt by Slovenia to secede.

The difference between secession and decolonization is that secession is defined by the independence of a piece of territory that had previously been regarded as an integral part of the territory of the parent state. In contrast, decolonization results in the independence of a territory that is geographically distant and demographically and constitutionally separate from the state that had previously been administering it. While the line between dissolution and secession can sometimes appear blurred, post-1945 decolonization is clearly understood to be a completely distinct category from secession in international relations and law. That said, as shall be seen later, the issues facing a newly decolonized state and a newly independent secessionist state are remarkably similar, if not largely the same.

What is free association?

One option that could be pursued by the remaining colonial territories that wish to seek independence but do not have the capabilities to take a full and active role on the international stage is free association with another state. Free association allows territories to have a very high degree of self-government, while ceding responsibility for certain key functions, such as defense and foreign policy, to another country.

In practice, free association is a fluid concept. In some circumstances, the state entering into free association with another may be recognized as a fully independent member of the UN. The most obvious examples are Palau, the Federated States of Micronesia, and the Marshall Islands. All have signed compacts of free association agreement with the United States, which provides for their defense while they each retain full control over foreign affairs—although they usually vote alongside the United States in the UN and other multilateral organizations.

At other times, the concept of free association can be rather less clear cut. For example, the small Pacific island territories of the Cook Islands and Niue are both classed as "self-governing states in free association with New Zealand." This means that both territories depend on New Zealand to manage their foreign policy and defense. Unlike the states in free association with the United States, neither is a full member of the UN. However, they are members of several UN bodies and institutions—including UNESCO, WHO, the Food and Agriculture Organization (FAO), and the International Civil Aviation Organization (ICAO)—and are recognized by the UN as having their own treaty-making capacity. They also conduct some diplomatic activities. For instance, Niue has its own permanent missions to the EU and the Cook Islands have a permanent representative at the International Maritime Organization (IMO). Furthermore, they also appear to retain full independence in terms of foreign policy decision making. This was highlighted in May and June 2015 when it was announced that the Cook Islands and Niue had decided to recognize Kosovo, even though New Zealand had done so six years earlier, in 2009.

Does a referendum need to be held to create a new state?

No. However, an interesting picture emerges when one looks at the uses of popular votes and the creation of new states. In cases of consensual secession, a referendum (or a plebiscite as it is also called) is often an intrinsic part of the independence process. This is because, as a rule, an act of secession will only be accepted by the international community if it is done with the express permission of the parent state. Where a state is willing to consider independence for a part of its territory, it will often want to ensure that this is the unambiguous wish of the inhabitants of that territory. The last three countries to join the UN—Eritrea on independence from Ethiopia (1993), Montenegro following its decision to leave the State Union with Serbia (2006), and South Sudan on independence from Sudan (2011)—all did so after a referendum. In cases of unilateral secession, the use of referendums is mixed. While Nagorno-Karabakh, Transnistria, and South Ossetia all held votes to secede from their parent states, Abkhazia and Northern Cyprus did not. Kosovo is an unusual case. Although it held a referendum on independence in 1991 that was only recognized by Albania, no popular vote occurred before its widely recognized declaration of independence in 2008.

In other situations, referendums have tended to be used in a rather erratic manner. Interestingly, in cases of state mergers, they have tended not to play a part. No vote was held when Egypt and Syria formed the UAR, nor was there a referendum when Tanganyika and Zanzibar united to form Tanzania. More recently, East and West Germany and North and South Yemen united without a popular vote. Likewise, many cases of decolonization took place without a formal vote by the population. None of the Portuguese or Belgian colonies that became independent were ever given a vote, and the only British colonies that became independent through a popular vote were Malta (1964) and Bahrain (1970). (Of course, informal plebiscites were occasionally organized to show the strength of feeling of the population against colonial rule. For example, the Greek Orthodox Church in Cyprus organized a vote in 1950 to gauge support for the island's union with Greece.) In contrast, all twenty of France's African colonies were given a say over the constitution establishing the Fifth Republic on the basis that a rejection would lead to independence. However, only one, Guinea, voted against the constitution and thus gained statehood. Thereafter, three more French territories gained statehood through a popular vote: Algeria (1962), Comoros (1974), and Djibouti (1977). More recently, the trend has been toward referendums. Again, the votes in New Caledonia and the Falkland Islands, which confirmed continued French and British rule respectively, are good cases in point.

In the case of state dissolution, the picture is also mixed. There was never a popular vote in Czechoslovakia. The decision to dissolve the state was reached by the political leaders and then carried through by the Federal Assembly. In the case of the Soviet Union, some republics—such as Armenia, Azerbaijan, Georgia, Turkmenistan, and Uzbekistan—held referendums. Others, such as Belarus, did not. In Yugoslavia, referendums played a major part in the disintegration process. The only republic that never held a vote, either officially or unofficially, was Serbia. The rest all did so at one point or another: Slovenia (1990), Kosovo (1991), Croatia (1991), Macedonia (1991), Bosnia and Herzegovina (1992), and Montenegro (2006). However, the Yugoslav case points to a danger of referendums. In cases where there are competing claims to statehood, popular votes can raise rather than resolve tensions. For instance, the referendums in Croatia and Bosnia were rejected by Croatian Serbs and Bosnian Serbs, who claimed that all-republic referendums could not constitutionally decide questions of independence. Meanwhile, the Croatian Serb and Bosnian Serb counter-referendums, in 1991, were in turn rejected by the governments of the two republics, and the international community. A referendum successfully settles contested claims only if the relevant parties agree on its validity and precise terms.

How are independence referendums organized?

There are in fact a wide range of issues that need to be considered when organizing an independence referendum. First and foremost, it needs to be acceptable to all relevant parties and the international community. A referendum called by one side without the support of the other will not be regarded as legitimate. If it is called just by the parent state, there will be questions as to whether it is a free and fair expression of the will of the people. If the vote is held by the territory seeking independence without the consent of the parent state, it will be rejected as a unilateral act.

Assuming the two sides do agree on a vote, they will need to agree on the question to put to voters. Will it be a straight choice between two outcomes, or between several choices? For example, in some of the referendums held in South Pacific states, as well as in Puerto Rico, people were given a range of choices, such as independence, free association, or becoming a part of the United States. Even where the choice is between independence or the status quo, the actual question can vary enormously. In Scotland, the question was simple: "Should Scotland be an independent country?" In contrast, the 1995 referendum in Quebec asked a far more complicated question: "Do you agree that Quebec should become sovereign after having made a formal offer to Canada for a new economic and political partnership within the scope of the bill respecting the future of Quebec and of the agreement signed on June 12, 1995?"

Then there is the question of who votes. Some believe that referendums should include the entire population of the parent state and the seceding territory. This is incorrect. By convention, it applies only to the self-determination unit and not to the population of the parent state as well. This has been the practice in all the most recent referendums on independence: Scotland, South Sudan, Montenegro, and Quebec. In each of these cases, the people of the rest of the United Kingdom, Sudan, Serbia, and Canada were not given a say in the decision. Nevertheless, some states, such as Spain and Ukraine, insist that any vote, even if permitted, must include the whole country. Then there are other questions as to who gets to vote. For example, in the case of Scotland it was decided that the voting roll should be the same as that for the Scottish Parliament. This meant that all EU citizens resident in Scotland could have a say. Often the question of whether to give the diaspora a vote can be crucial. For example, Montenegro permitted its citizens living abroad to vote. However, Montenegrins living in Serbia, the partner country in the state union, were denied the right to participate. This clearly swung the vote in favor of independence as it was widely understood that the country's large community in Serbia would have voted to retain the state union.

There are also questions over the conduct of the vote, such as the timing of the polls and the participation of international observers. While the vote may take place on a specific day, in some cases it could be held over several days. The vote in South Sudan took place over six days.

Finally, there is the issue of what constitutes a result in favor of secession. Is there is a necessary minimum turnout? And is the vote decided by a simple majority? In the Scottish case, it was 50 percent of all those voting. In the Montenegrin example, the EU-mediated agreement stipulated that the vote would only pass if it achieved 55 percent support for independence on a minimum 50 percent turnout. This was done to ensure that there was clear support for the outcome in the hope that this would minimize the risk of tension in the aftermath of the vote.

What are continuator and successor states?

In any case of secession, it is important to define the legal relationship between the parties. For this reason, the terms continuator and successor states have emerged. In cases of secession, the parent state usually retains its rights and legal personality. It is therefore known in international law as the continuator state. On the other hand, the seceding state is generally a new entity and is called the successor state. However, with mergers and dissolutions, the situation can often be rather more confusing. For instance, when Czechoslovakia split, the Czech Republic and Slovakia decided that neither would claim to be the continuator state. Both would be new entities and thus successors. In more complex cases, one state may emerge by agreement as the continuator state. This happened with the

Soviet Union. In that case, Russia was the continuator state, whereas most of the other republics, except for the three Baltic republics (which were regarded as not having been legally a part of the Soviet Union at the time of its dissolution), were successor states.

The questions of continuation and succession matter because they influence a wide variety of issues, such as membership of international bodies, treaty obligations, and state property and debts. Membership of international organizations is especially crucial for the relations of new states with third parties. Perhaps the most valuable status in international politics is permanent membership of the UN Security Council. When the Soviet Union dissolved, it was relatively quickly decided that Russia would retain the Soviet seat on the council. Another interesting example was Yugoslavia. When the country collapsed, the Federal Republic of Yugoslavia (FRY) claimed to be the continuator state. However, this was rejected by the other republics. In September 1992, the UN Security Council decided that the SFRY had "ceased to exist" and the FRY's claim to continue to be a UN member was "not generally accepted." The FRY was therefore required to apply for membership.[1] For the next eight years it refused to do so (although, interestingly, it could participate in various UN organs in place of the SFRY). However, in 2000, under a new government, the FRY relented and was admitted to the UN as a new member.

It was in response to the complexities of the issue that the Vienna Convention on Succession of States in Respect of Treaties (1978) and the Vienna Convention on Succession of States in Respect of State Property, Archives, and Debts (1983) were concluded. However, their effects are limited. While the first convention came into force in 1996, only twenty-three countries are parties to it. These include the six republics of Yugoslavia and, perhaps rather interestingly as it faces a

1. United Nations Security Council Resolution 777, September 19, 1992.

secessionist challenge, Cyprus. Additionally, nineteen more states are signatories, but have not yet ratified it. The second convention has not yet come into force. The limited impact of the conventions shows that there are relatively few established rules of succession. A lot depends on the negotiations among the parties. This means that there can be very different outcomes across cases. Where there is no agreement among the relevant parties on matters of succession, the position of the international community on issues is usually decisive until some sort of agreement is reached.

How are the borders of new states demarcated?

Prior to decolonization, there was no universal principle of border making beyond the general preference that borders should delineate the new state as it had been effectively established on the ground. The question of the new international borders would be settled at independence. Since decolonization, and as noted in Chapter 4, the international community has embraced the principle that the legitimacy of the land and sea boundaries as they existed prior to independence should be respected—*uti possidetis juris*. In many circumstances, the demarcation of boundaries is therefore a relatively straightforward process. The borders of the new state will match its administrative boundaries prior to statehood. However, occasionally a problem may arise because no such boundaries previously existed. This can cause serious administrative problems, such as over legal jurisdiction and law enforcement. More seriously, they can lead to armed conflict. (Although, it has to be stressed that not all border issues can cause major problems or need to be resolved. Many states can peacefully coexist with border differences. Even the United States and Canada have outstanding territorial disagreements.)

A more contentious issue can be maritime boundaries. This is because states will often not delineate their boundaries between their domestic constituent parts. So, a newly independent territory can have a clearly demarcated land border with its parent state but suddenly find that it has a serious maritime issue. In many cases, these can be relatively easily determined according to standing practices of international law. However, here too disputes can arise. One such case is Slovenia and Croatia, which have a long standing and unresolved maritime dispute in the Adriatic Sea.

There are a variety of ways border disputes can be resolved. Sometimes, they can be settled by negotiation. In 2016, Belgium and the Netherlands agreed to swap land after the course of a river was changed, which left each country with bits of territory on the wrong side of the waterway.[2] Alternatively, the disputing states may request external mediation, by either a mutually acceptable third country or an outside body, such as the UN. Another way is to pursue a legal solution. The Permanent Court of Arbitration, founded in 1899, has dealt with many boundary issues. Some of these have had considerable significance. In 1913, it decided on the border between the Dutch and Portuguese colonial territories on the island of Timor. This was to have major implications later as it formed the border between Indonesia and what is now the independent state of East Timor. More recently, the court has helped to resolve the border dispute between Ethiopia and Eritrea, following the latter's independence in 1993 after a thirty-year war. Finally, the International Court of Justice can also hear border and maritime boundary disputes. Both parties, however, must be UN member states, and both must consent to the dispute being settled in that court.

2. "Belgium and the Netherlands Swap Land, and Remain Friends," *The New York Times*, November 28, 2016.

How are state assets and liabilities divided?

As well as determining borders, there are a whole range of practical issues that need to be addressed when a territory secedes or a country dissolves. One of the most potentially difficult and contentious issues in any negotiation process can be the division of state assets and liabilities. Where the split is essentially amicable, this can be a relatively easy process. For example, the Czech Republic and Slovakia concluded the basic negotiations within a matter of weeks. At other times, it can be a long and tortuous process that may even require outside mediation. For example, it took almost a decade for the initial five republics of the SFRY (Serbia and Montenegro were still united as the Federal Republic of Yugoslavia at that stage) to reach an agreement.[3] And even when an agreement is reached, disputes may arise later over implementation.

In general, there are three classes of assets that need to be divided up: movable and immovable property; financial assets; and diplomatic assets. The first of these, movable and immovable property, includes a range of state holdings, such as government offices and military bases. In many cases, this can be easy to settle. In the case of immovable property, the parties may simply decide that it is retained by the state on whose territory it is located. If the facility is of significant national importance, other arrangements can sometimes be reached. For example, in the case of military bases, there may be a leasing arrangement whereby the parent state continues to operate the base for a certain number of years. In some cases, sovereignty over the territory can be retained. For example, when Cyprus became independent in 1960, Britain retained 99 square miles of territory in perpetuity as sovereign military bases and was granted use of a further number of sites that formally passed

3. "Agreement on Succession Issues," Vienna, May 25, 2001, https:// treaties.un.org/doc/source/recenttexts/29-1.pdf.

to the new Republic of Cyprus.[4] In the case of movable state property, this can pose greater problems. This category can include a great number of items, ranging from military hardware through to cultural items. Military items can often be a source of considerable negotiation, as these are often high value. Artwork and historical items can also be problematic since they may be held by one of the parties but originate from or have intrinsic significance to the other.

The second area to be decided is financial assets. These can include an array of different items. Decisions will need to be reached on how to divide up items such as the financial assets of government departments, central bank holdings, foreign currency holdings, shares and bonds, reserves of gold and other precious metals, assets held in foreign banks and international institutions, and sums owed to the country by external parties. Another issue that needs to be decided is how to tackle the question of financial quotas and drawing rights in international financial institutions. This is important since the decision can then determine how much the new state will have to pay to be a member of those institutions.

Next, agreement needs to be reached on the division of diplomatic properties, including embassies, residences, and consular offices. In some cases, this is not an issue. A new state may decide to forego any claim to existing diplomatic assets and simply makes its own way in the world by acquiring its own facilities. For instance, when the Soviet Union collapsed, Russia took control of all the old state's embassies around the world. The rest of the republics then established their own missions. In other cases, an amicable agreement can be quickly reached. For instance, when Czechoslovakia split, the large embassy in London was simply divided between the two new countries. To this day, the Czech Republic and Slovakia share

---

4. Treaty Concerning the Establishment of the Republic of Cyprus, Signed at Nicosia, on August 16, 1960.

the same building. At other times, it can be an extremely contentious process. It took many years for the states of the former Yugoslavia to reach an agreement on diplomatic properties. In the end, they were parceled out among the republics, with Serbia taking the most and Slovenia the least based on a percentage formula.

Then there are state records, such as registries of births, deaths, and marriages as well as land registries (more officially known as cadastral records). In some cases, these may already be handled on a devolved basis, such as at a local municipality or provincial level. In such cases, this question can be resolved with little or no difficulty. However, at other times a centralized system may exist, and resolution could require extensive discussions. Another important issue is the question of national archives. Most states will want to maintain a record of their history. However, the parent state or former colonial power may not want to give up their records. In these cases, it is sometimes possible to resolve the issue by providing the new state with copies of the relevant documents.

As well as decisions on how to divide state assets, there are important questions of liabilities. New states not only come into being bearing some of the assets of the parent state, they will often also inherit a proportion of their debt. These debts could be to other countries and international financial institutions or may be money owed to commercial creditors, such as banks. Again, some of this may be relatively easy to determine. For example, a new state could agree to assume the burden of paying for an infrastructure project on its territory. But what happens if this project crosses the border between states or is in one state but produces benefits for the other (such as an irrigation project)? Then there are debts that are owed by the state that cannot simply be passed to one state or the other. In these cases, an agreement needs to be reached as to how to apportion liability.

One of the most important issues that must be resolved is the question of pensions. Very often citizens from one state may have spent a period working in another and paying into the pension system. What happens when they return to their home state? In the case of Yugoslavia, an agreement was reached that meant that citizens from each republic who had worked in another republic would be entitled to a state pension from that republic at a level proportional to the amount of time they had worked there. In a country where people often moved around, it is not unusual for people to be claiming pensions from three or four of the former republics.

As well as assets and liabilities, there are many other practical issues that need to be discussed. For example, what happens to officials who find themselves in the "wrong" state? While some may want to return to their "home" country, others may not want to do so as they may have established ties to the country in which they now work. Sometimes, they may be offered citizenship. However, their birth nationality may affect their access to sensitive documents. And what about members of the armed forces stationed in the country? Do they have to leave and return to their home state or are they permitted to stay and join the armed forces of the new state if they so wish? In cases where they must return to their "home" state, this can lead to odd situations. Consider naval officers who originated from Serbia. Following Montenegro's independence, they had to return to serve in a landlocked country.

Who becomes a citizen of the new state?

One of the more contentious issues that can arise is the question of citizenship. In many cases, a new state will simply extend citizenship to anyone either born or living in their territory at the time of independence. However, sometimes the granting of citizenship can prove to be a politically charged issue. For example, at the time when they reasserted their independence, many ethnic Russians were living in the three Baltic republics. In Lithuania, where Russians accounted for about 10 percent of the population, a decision was taken to grant citizenship to all those living in the country at the time of independence. In contrast, neither Estonia nor Latvia automatically granted citizenship to people who had moved to the country during Soviet rule. Ethnic minorities had to take language tests to prove that they were sufficiently well integrated. As a result, hundreds of thousands of Russian speakers were denied citizenship. Although this figure has dropped, there are still many tens of thousands who have not acquired Latvian or Estonian citizenship and face stringent language tests to acquire it. At other times, administrative issues have caused major problems. For example, Slovenia denied citizenship to thousands of people born elsewhere in Yugoslavia who failed to meet the deadline to apply for citizenship after independence and even destroyed their documents when they did show up to apply after the cut-off point. To this day, many of these so-called "erased" have still not obtained Slovenian citizenship.

Another problematic issue that often arises is dual citizenship. Some new states, to build up a national identity, take a very restrictive approach and demand that their citizens renounce their ties to any other country. For example, Montenegro imposed stringent restrictions on dual citizenship, largely due to concerns about the loyalties of the third of its population that identifies as ethnic Serb. Other countries, especially those with a large diaspora community, take a far more relaxed approach and accept dual nationality to encourage closer ties with members of the community living overseas. Indeed, this can often be an important way of securing political and financial support for a new country from its overseas community. In such cases, policies vary widely regarding who can gain citizenship through descent (*jus sanguinis*, right of blood). Sometimes, this is merely extended to the children of those born in the country or entitled to citizenship at independence. Other countries have adopted looser criteria, merely requiring a person to prove that they had at least one grandparent born there. In the case of Italy, citizenship can be extended to anyone who can prove that they are descended from someone who was an Italian citizen when the Italian state came into being, in 1861. In some cases, the citizenship criteria are even more broadly conceived. Israel will extend citizenship to anyone of the Jewish faith, either by birth or conversion, who immigrates to Israel.[5]

What institutions does a new state need?

As well as determining the terms of its independence, a new state must plan for when it formally assumes sovereignty. This means deciding on a political system and drawing up a constitution, which raises any number of questions. Will it be a unitary state, a federation, or even a confederation? What sort of constitutional system will it adopt? Will it be a presidential system or a parliamentary one? How will the head of state be selected? Even the mechanisms for answering these questions require decisions as there are various procedures that can be chosen. For example, the state institutions could be created by a consultative process involving politicians and other eminent figures or by a specially convened constitutional convention. They could even be drafted by the departing state or an external commission.

The new state will also need a government and civil service. Very often, many of the core functions of statehood are likely to exist and the changeover following independence may be as minor as simply changing the plaques on the outside of buildings. However, this is not always the case. During the period of decolonization, many new states were woefully

5. "Citizenship," Government of Montenegro, https://www.gov.me/en/article/citizenship; "Citizenship," Ministry of Foreign Affairs and International Cooperation, Italy, http://www.esteri.it/mae/en/italiani_nel_mondo/serviziconsolari/cittadinanza.html; "The Law of Return," The Jewish Agency for Israel, https://archive.jewishagency.org/first-steps/program/5131.

unprepared for statehood. The most notorious example was the Congo, which became independent from Belgium in June 1960. It had barely any university graduates and almost no Congolese had been given any meaningful administrative experience. Today, such situations are unusual. In the contemporary era, state creation is rarely a process that starts from nothing. Almost all new states have had some form of self-government prior to independence or received considerable support from external parties before assuming statehood. However, such experience and support are certainly not a guarantee of post-independence success. South Sudan, the most recent state to become independent, in 2011, has become a failed state.

As for executive functions, the assumption is that the new state will assume the bare minimum of competences at independence. This is usually understood to mean ministries to handle finance, education, and healthcare. However, other ministries that one would often expect to see would include defense, foreign affairs, development, agriculture, social security, industry, transport, communication, justice, natural resources, maritime affairs, employment, business, infrastructure, youth, tourism, sport, and culture. Obviously, many small states combine some of these functions either within a single ministry or by appointing a minister to several roles. For example, Nauru has just six ministers. Contrast this with the United States, which has fifteen federal executive departments, or the United Kingdom, which has twenty-three ministerial departments. Of course, the number of ministries can also reflect the political system in place. Federations usually devolve many powers to subnational or regional administrations. Likewise, most territories will have their own police forces and court structures. In addition to the central government departments, there are a range of other bodies and institutions that states may have or will often want to develop. These include various regulatory agencies, a national broadcaster, and so on.

Can states share institutions?

While many institutions will be unique to the new state, it is not unknown that certain bodies or structures continue to be shared with the former parent state or colonial power, or even with neighboring states. This has long been seen in judicial matters, particularly at a high level. Twelve independent states—Brunei and several Caribbean and Pacific island states—use the British Judicial Committee of the Privy Council, in one form or another, as their highest court of appeal. However, this is starting to change. Some countries that once used the privy council now use the Caribbean Court of Justice. Likewise, in recent years, there has been a trend for countries to share embassies and diplomatic services. For example, Canada and Australia have a long-standing agreement to provide consular services to one another's citizens in places where the other is not represented. Similarly, EU citizens from any of the twenty-seven member states can seek consular help from an embassy of any of the other members. In the run-up to the independence referendum, the Scottish government announced that it would be open to sharing diplomatic missions with the rest of the United Kingdom.

Perhaps the most interesting shared institution is a head of state. To this day, fifteen members of the UN retain Queen Elizabeth II, as their sovereign.[6] In such cases, the queen is usually represented on a day-to-day basis by a resident governor-general. In recent years, some states have started to question whether this practice should continue. There is a feeling in some quarters that it would be more appropriate to become republics with their own citizens as heads of state. In 1999, Australia rejected the idea in a national referendum

6. As well as the United Kingdom, these are Antigua and Barbuda, Australia, The Bahamas, Belize, Canada, Grenada, Jamaica, New Zealand, Papua New Guinea, Saint Kitts and Nevis, Saint Lucia, Saint Vincent and the Grenadines, Solomon Islands, and Tuvalu.

(55–45 percent). More recently, Jamaica has raised the issue.[7] And on November 30, 2021, Barbados became the most recent country to replace the queen and become a republic. Another example, albeit unusual, of a country that shares a head of state is Andorra. Its co-princes are the president of France and the bishop of Urgell, in Spain.

Does a state need its own currency?

For many states, a national currency is an intrinsic symbol of sovereignty. Most new countries want to issue their own banknotes and coins. However, there is no formal requirement for a state to have its own currency. In fact, around a quarter of UN members do not have their own separate national currency. In some cases, a group of states may forego having individual currencies and instead enter a currency union. The most obvious example is the euro, which is used by nineteen members of the EU. Another example is the Eastern Caribbean dollar. This is used by six independent states—Antigua and Barbuda, Dominica, Grenada, Saint Kitts and Nevis, Saint Lucia, and Saint Vincent and the Grenadines—as well as by Anguilla and Montserrat, both of which are British Overseas Territories. The Central African (CFA) franc is used by eight West African states: Benin, Burkina Faso, Guinea-Bissau, Ivory Coast, Mali, Niger, Senegal, and Togo.

Another option is for a country to use the currency of another state, either formally or informally. The most obvious are the six states that have adopted the US dollar: Ecuador and El Salvador in Central America; East Timor and the Marshall Islands, Micronesia, and Palau in the Pacific. Other examples include Kiribati, Nauru, and Tuvalu, which use the Australian dollar. Lesotho, Namibia, and Swaziland use the South African

---

7. "Jamaica unveils plan to ditch Queen as head of state," *The Telegraph*, April 16, 2016.

rand. The Cook Islands and Niue use the New Zealand dollar. In Europe, Liechtenstein uses the Swiss franc. Then there are the six European states that are not part of the EU but have opted to use the euro as their official currency. Four have done so with the permission of the EU: Andorra, Monaco, San Marino, and the Vatican. The other two, Kosovo and Montenegro, have done so unilaterally.

Most usually, de facto states will not try to establish their own currency. Instead, they will often use the currency of their patron state or a widely accepted international currency. For example, Northern Cyprus uses the Turkish lira, Nagorno-Karabakh uses the Armenian dram, and South Ossetia and Abkhazia both use the Russian ruble. The one notable exception to this is Somaliland, which introduced the Somaliland shilling in 1994. However, the Somali shilling is also widely used.

Does a state need its own military?

Although a military has often been a key symbol of statehood, not all countries maintain armed forces. In fact, there are at least fourteen UN member states that do not have any formal military capabilities at all. Perhaps the most famous of these are Iceland, which got rid of its army in 1869, and Costa Rica, which abolished its army in 1949. However, there are also other states—particularly island states in the Pacific and the Caribbean—that have also chosen to forego a standing military force.

Of course, this rarely means that a country will have no security capabilities. In most cases, even if it does not have a formal defense force, a country will maintain paramilitary police units for internal security purposes. At the same time, external defense will usually be covered by some sort of arrangement. Sometimes, this may be an agreement with an outside power. For instance, the United States provides security for the Marshall Islands, New Zealand has an agreement to defend Samoa, and Monaco is defended by France. At other times, there may be a collective defense arrangement in place. For example, Iceland is a member of NATO. In the case of the three Eastern Caribbean states without armed forces (Grenada, St. Lucia, and Saint Vincent and the Grenadines) defense is provided through the Regional Security System, which is a partnership between Caribbean Community (CARICOM) members, the United States, Canada, Brazil, the United Kingdom, and the Dutch, French, and UK overseas territories in the region. There are also examples of shared permanent military institutions. The United States and Canada have a long-standing joint air defense organization, NORAD (North American Aerospace Defense Command).

One rare, but particularly important, defense question arising from secession relates to the ownership of nuclear weapons. To date, this issue has only come up in one situation: the disintegration of the Soviet Union. In that case, the decision was taken by the new states that the only country that would continue to have nuclear weapons was the Russian Federation. In return for relinquishing its access to a nuclear deterrent, Ukraine accepted a system whereby Russia, the United Kingdom, and the United States would affirm to respect its sovereignty and independence. (Albeit not particularly well in the end.) However, this question also arose in the debate over Scotland's independence. In this case, the ruling Scottish National Party announced that an independent Scotland would be free of nuclear weapons and any on Scottish soil would be moved elsewhere in the United Kingdom. The problem is that the main UK naval base for nuclear submarines was based in Scotland and could not be readily moved. In the event of another referendum on Scottish independence, this is again likely to be major point of discussion.

What symbols of statehood are needed?

In addition to the institutions of statehood, a new state also needs to acquire the traditional symbols of independence.

Perhaps the most obvious is a flag and a national anthem. Given the importance of a national flag, countries will want to ensure that they hold some significance, for example by the use of a color scheme or through the inclusion of a specific national emblem. (Interestingly, Cyprus and Kosovo are the only two countries that include a map of their state on their flag.) Sometimes national flags will share similar elements with other states to emphasize a common ethnic or political heritage. For instance, the flags of New Zealand and Australia, among others, include the British Union flag in their design. Many Arab states use green, red, white, and black color schemes, just as many Slavic states use variations of the red, white, and blue horizontal tricolor. (The flags of Slovakia and Slovenia are particularly alike—further compounding the difficulties many outsiders have in differentiating between them.) The flags of neighbors Romania and Moldova, which share ethnic ties, are differentiated solely by a crest on the latter. Matters are made even more confusing as the Romanian flag is almost identical to Chad's—no relation.

Likewise, national anthems can become iconic symbols of a nation. Consider the Unites States' "The Star-Spangled Banner," France's "La Marseillaise," or Germany's "Lied der Deutschen." Like flags, national anthems are varied. Some are based on a traditional national tune or song. Others are composed especially for the new state, such as "All Hail Liberia," written for its independence in 1847, or "Sons and Daughters of Saint Lucia" and "Saint Vincent, Land so Beautiful," written for their independence in 1979. In divided societies, the anthem may be deliberately designed to have a unifying effect. For example, South Africa's anthem contains verses in five of the country's national languages. Switzerland has four entirely different sets of lyrics, written in French, German, Italian, and Romansch. However, anthems are not always unique to a country. The United Kingdom's "God Save the Queen" and Liechtenstein's "Oben am jungen Rhein" share the same tune.

Cyprus has two anthems. It shares the national anthems of Greece and Turkey, though without the words.

As well as the traditional symbols of statehood, there are many other ways a country will want to assert its presence on the international stage. One of the most important is fielding sports teams. For many countries, a national soccer team is a particularly significant symbol of their identity. Likewise, many countries also have a strong sense of pride when their flag is paraded at the Olympic Games. (Although, technically, statehood is not a formal requirement for membership of either FIFA or the International Olympic Committee.[8]) Beyond these, there are any number of other symbols that have significance for a country. For instance, a national airline has often been an important symbol of statehood, although perhaps less so now than it once was. In principle, there are no limits as to what can serve a symbol of statehood: postage stamps; flora and fauna (many countries have a national animal or plant); national dishes and beverages; natural wonders; historic monuments; or significant achievement of the social, economic, and political system have all been used to embody countries.

8. The International Olympic Committee includes the national Olympic committees of 206 countries. This is made up of the 193 UN members, as well as American Samoa, Aruba, Bermuda, Cayman Islands, Chinese Taipei, Cook Islands, Guam, Hong Kong (China), Kosovo, Palestine, Puerto Rico, Virgin Islands (British), and Virgin Islands (US). FIFA membership of 211 countries consists of every UN member except Kiribati, Marshall Islands, Micronesia, Monaco, Nauru, Palau, Tuvalu, and the United Kingdom, which plays as four separate countries: England, Scotland, Wales, and Northern Ireland. The other members include American Samoa, Anguilla, Aruba, Bermuda, British Virgin Islands, Cayman Islands, Chinese Taipei, Cook Islands, Curacao, Faroe Islands, Gibraltar, Guam, Hong Kong, Kosovo, Macau, Montserrat, New Caledonia, Palestine, Puerto Rico, Tahiti, Turks and Caicos, and US Virgin Islands.

How long does it take to become independent?

It all depends. Even in cases of consensual secession or dissolution there is no standard length of time needed. In some cases, the informal or formal preparations for statehood may have been taking place for a long time. At other times, the process of voting for independence or gaining agreement from the parent state can mark the start of what can become a very lengthy process of negotiation. As well as defining the terms of separation and establishing the functioning structures of statehood, steps must be taken to assume responsibility for such matters as the issuing and distribution of a new currency, if needed, and assuming the country's place on the world stage and in regional and international organizations (discussed in Chapter 6).

Nevertheless, in some instances the gap between a referendum on independence and actual statehood can be very short indeed. For example, in the case of Serbia and Montenegro, which had effectively been operating as two separate states for several years, it was an extremely quick process. The referendum was held on May 21, 2006, and the declaration of independence came just a few weeks later. In South Sudan, the independence referendum was held January 9–15, and independence was declared on July 9, six-months later. In other cases, the process can be lengthier. If Scotland had voted for independence, Scottish officials said that they would have expected the process to have been completed within eighteen months.

Can a country change its name after independence?

Yes. There have in fact been many instances where states have changed their names. In some cases, this has been done to reflect a change in political circumstances but has not actually affected the common name of the country. For example, in 1981, Iran changed its name from Iran to the Islamic Republic of Iran. At other times, a name change can be more substantial, for instance, Siam became Thailand (1949), Dahomey became Benin (1974), Upper Volta became Burkina Faso (1984), Ceylon became Sri Lanka (1991), and Swaziland became Eswatini (2018). However, perhaps the most famous name change occurred in early 2019, when the Republic of Macedonia became the Republic of North Macedonia following a deal with neighboring Greece to end a twenty-seven-year dispute that had seen the country admitted to the UN under a provisional name: the former Yugoslav Republic of Macedonia (FYROM).

In most cases, name changes are relatively easy. The UN merely needs to be notified. Sometimes, however, it can raise political issues. An obvious example is Burma's 1989 change of name to Myanmar. Although the UN now lists the country as Myanmar, and this is recognized by the large majority of UN members, the United States continues to use Burma. The United Kingdom, the former colonial power, uses both as Myanmar (Burma). The US refusal to accept the name change is because the name was changed by the unelected military junta and had not been supported by the pro-democracy opposition. As a US State Department official put it, "our concern . . . is not the name itself as much as the process of how the decision was made to change the official name from Burma to Myanmar."[9]

Can a state change its national anthem and flag?

Although flags and anthems are important symbols of statehood, they too sometimes change. This may be done to mark a transition between one era and another. For example, Georgia changed its flag in 2004 following the Rose Revolution that deposed the previous government. Bosnia and Herzegovina and Kosovo changed their flags following external pressures

9. "Background Briefing on Burma," US State Department, April 4, 2012.

from states backing their independence to suggest ethnic inclusivity of the republics. Sometimes it is done to assert a more distinct identity. Several states that retain the British Union flag within their designs have decided to change them. An early example was Canada, which adopted its current maple leaf design in 1965. However, New Zealand, whose flag bears a confusing similarity to that of Australia, rejected a new design in a national referendum held in 2016.

Then there are cases of states that revert to an earlier flag. One interesting example is the Czech Republic. Prior to the dissolution of Czechoslovakia, it floated the idea of adopting a new red and white flag. However, once independent, it decided to continue using the old Czechoslovak flag, even though this had been prohibited under an agreement reached with Slovakia at the time of independence. Another case is Malawi. It used a tricolor with a rising sun from its independence, in 1964, until 2010, when it altered the flag to show a full sun. This was meant to signify that it was now a full state. However, in 2012, the parliament decided to readopt the original flag. Similarly, national anthems can also revert to an earlier version. After the fall of the Soviet Union, Russia adopted a new anthem. However, the old one was reintroduced, albeit with new lyrics, in 2000.

6

JOINING THE INTERNATIONAL COMMUNITY

How does recognition happen?

Having gained independence, the priority for any new state is to join the international community. The first step in this process is obtaining recognition from other countries. In terms of the formal act of recognition, this can be done in a variety of different ways. At its simplest, a senior official with the necessary authority—whether it be the president, prime minister, or foreign minister—makes the decision and an announcement is made, for example by a letter to the foreign ministry or to a relevant official or even with something as simple as a press release. As one might expect, this is the most common form of recognition. However, there are several other methods of recognition, such as the exchange of diplomatic representatives or the upgrading of an existing mission, such as a consulate, into an embassy. Another way is for an official from the recognizing state to attend the independence ceremony of a new state. Alternatively, a letter or some other form of communication from an official of the territory seeking recognition may receive an official reply that leaves little doubt that it is now accepted as a state. Finally, recognition can be signaled through the signing of a bilateral treaty. But this can be problematic. In cases where the treaty specifically covers diplomatic or political relations, there is little room for confusion. The problem is that certain nonpolitical agreements covering matters such as travel documents might not necessarily amount to formal recognition. If a country subsequently insists that it had no intention to recognize a territory by signing a nonpolitical agreement, then it is hard to argue that it did in fact recognize it.

Although recognition is usually a straightforward procedure, this is not always the case. For example, recognition does not have to be formally stated. It can be implied. Sometimes, a country will not make a formal statement of recognition. Rather it is up to other states to draw their own conclusions based on how the state in question interacts with the other state. This can give rise to considerable confusion. At what point does engagement with a territory become actual recognition of statehood? Perhaps the best example of how such a situation can lead to problems was New Zealand's decision in 2008 not to take a formal position on Kosovo's declaration of independence. Instead, the prime minister announced that Auckland's stance would become clear over time. Given the intensity of the recognition issue, this inevitably led to constant speculation as to whether New Zealand could be added to the list of countries that had recognized Kosovo. In the end, the government gave in and formally announced that it had recognized Kosovo.[1] Fortunately, implied recognition tends to be rather rare. Most states prefer to be clear about their policies, especially in cases of contested statehood.

Can a state be forced to recognize another state?

No. Recognition is a wholly sovereign decision. States are at liberty to choose whether, when, how, and why they recognize another state. Moreover, no state is under an obligation to recognize another state, even if every other country in the world

1. "Kosovo: PM explains why no formal statement from NZ," *New Zealand Herald*, February 18, 2008; "New Zealand recognizes Kosovo," *Balkan Insight*, November 9, 2009.

has done so. As John Foster Dulles, a US secretary of state, noted, "diplomatic recognition is always a privilege, never a right." If a state does not want to recognize another state, there is no way to require it to do so—although it may face considerable pressure to do so from other states.

Likewise, states cannot be prevented from recognizing territories as states even if others do not. Most usually, countries will want their decision to be in line with established legal and political principles. However, if a country wants to recognize another state it is free to do so and is under no legal obligation to justify its decision. Nor can a state's decision to recognize another state be annulled or declared invalid by a third party. For example, the UN Security Council may condemn a declaration of independence and call on states not to recognize a state that has unilaterally declared independence. However, it cannot reverse a recognition decision taken by one of its members. This has been seen very clearly with Turkey's continuing recognition of Northern Cyprus despite UN Security Council Resolution 541 calling on states not to recognize it.

What is collective recognition?

Although bilateral state-to-state recognition is the most usual form of recognition, sometimes a group of countries will choose to act together. This is known as collective recognition. Like bilateral recognition, this can take several forms. In historical terms, collective recognition has sometimes played a decisive role in the creation of new states. On occasion, groups of states would sometimes come together with the express intention of considering the acceptance of a new state, a process known as "recognition by conference." A good example of this was the recognition of Albania at the 1912–1913 London Conference. However, this method is now obsolete.

A more relevant form of collective recognition occurs when a state is included in a multilateral treaty. While the text may include an express declaration of recognition, more usually recognition is indicated through the mere inclusion of the state being recognized as a party to the treaty. However, as with the signing of a bilateral treaty, the acceptance of a treaty by various parties does not necessarily mean that they recognize one another. For instance, President Kennedy explicitly noted that the inclusion of East Germany in the 1963 Nuclear Test Ban Treaty did not amount to recognition of the country by the United States.[2] Alternatively, a state may be invited to take part in a multilateral meeting of some sort. Yet again, while such an invitation may amount to recognition, this cannot be taken for granted. For example, a mechanism exists to permit officials from states that do not recognize each other to take part in events by ensuring that no formal titles or symbols of state-hood are used. This way of holding meetings is sometimes re-ferred to as the Gymnich formula and is named after informal meetings of EU ministers at which no binding decisions are taken, the first of which was held at Gymnich Castle near Bonn. Lastly, collective recognition can occur when a state is admitted into an organization that is exclusively composed of other states. In such cases, the states agreeing to the admission of the new state are understood to have accepted its sovereign status. But even here there is room for confusion. Sometimes states have been admitted into organizations, such as the UN, even though some members may not recognize them.

More recently, however, "collective recognition" has tended to be used to describe a process whereby a group of coun-tries, often within a single international organization, take a joint decision on recognition. A good example of this was the EU's statement congratulating the people of South Sudan on their independence, in July 2011.[3] Although many indi-vidual members chose to issue their own separate statements

---

2. President John F. Kennedy, News Conference 59, August 1, 1963.
3. "Declaration by the EU and its Member States on the Republic of South Sudan's Independence, 9 July 2011," 12679/11, European Union, July 9, 2011.

of recognition, or even sent representatives to the independence ceremony, the joint statement amounted to collective recognition. Crucially, it is important to differentiate collective recognition from a process of collective consultation leading to individual acts of recognition, as occurred in the case of Kosovo. The United States and key members of the EU worked closely with one another, as well as with Pristina, in the run-up to declaration of independence. However, their subsequent recognition announcements were made individually.

Can recognition be subject to conditions?

While some lawyers argue that recognition should not be subject to conditions, historically states have nevertheless often attached conditions to recognition—even when the territory in question clearly qualified for recognition as a state. While the nature of these conditions has varied, they have invariably been justified in terms of the interests of international society. Indeed, such conditions have often reflected wider international concerns of the time. For example, among the first conditions attached to recognition was the British request that Brazil renounce the slave trade as it established de facto independence from Portugal in 1825. (The slave trade was outlawed by an international treaty in 1815 and the only country bucking this "standard of civilization" since then had been Portugal and its overseas territories. The United States had outlawed the importation of slaves in 1807.)

Perhaps the most prominent condition in the nineteenth and early twentieth centuries was respect for minority rights. This was presented to Greece and other Balkan states in the nineteenth century and to all the new states at the Paris Peace Conference in 1919. The condition was justified on the grounds of both "civilization" and international security. National and regional minorities were to be treated fairly as a matter of civilized conduct and to avert conflicts within new states that could pose external threats. Perhaps the best-known conditions in recent times were those imposed on former Yugoslav and Soviet republics in the early 1990s. They included commitments to minority rights, human rights, democracy, and disarmament.

Conditions attached to recognition have tended to be controversial as new states would often argue that they were subject to demands that not all existing states, and especially major powers, themselves embraced. Still, whatever one's view of conditionality, it seems likely to persist. New states have never successfully argued that they have a right to unconditional recognition. Indeed, the practice of conditionality confirms that new states enter an exclusive club with rules of membership and conduct rather than a natural community to which they are entitled to belong.

Can a state be "de-recognized"?

Another question that sometimes arises is whether a country can withdraw its recognition from another state. This is an issue that has long divided international lawyers. Some believe that withdrawing recognition from a state is not possible. Once granted, recognition becomes a binding legal commitment. The possibility of withdrawing it would create uncertainty in the international system. Others argue that it is possible if the circumstances that led to recognition change. What has tended to unite the two sides is the belief that a state cannot simply withdraw recognition and say that it does not recognize any legal authority over the territory in question. There can be no such thing today as terra nullius (nobody's land). One state or another must have sovereignty. Therefore, instead of "de-recognition," it is perhaps better to think of switching recognition.

In practical terms, there have been cases of recognition being transferred in this way. Tuvalu and Vanuatu both recognized Abkhazia and South Ossetia but later decided to accept Georgia's sovereignty over the two territories. More interestingly, if not bizarrely, Nauru recognized Abkhazia before deciding to once again accept Georgia's sovereignty over the territory, before repeating the process again. At present, its position remains unclear. Also, in the run-up to the International Court of Justice advisory opinion on Kosovo there were suggestions that if the court ruled explicitly in Serbia's favor some countries would be willing to re-recognize Serbia's sovereignty over the territory. This did not happen. However, since 2018, at least fifteen countries have in fact withdrawn their recognition of Kosovo following a campaign by Serbia (the precise number is contested as some countries have put forward unclear or contradictory statements). In this sense, while de-recognition is possible, it only arises in cases of contested sovereignty where there are two claimants to a territory.

How do countries establish diplomatic relations?

While recognition is about accepting the existence of another sovereign state, establishing diplomatic relations is about creating a formal relationship with that state. Although recognition and the establishment of diplomatic relations often run together, they are in fact two separate processes. Indeed, there are many cases where two countries recognize each other, but do not have diplomatic relations. This may be due to outstanding issues that need to be resolved first, or just because there is no pressing need to establish formal direct ties.

Even after they have been established, diplomatic relations can be downgraded or even severed. This usually happens after a major incident between the two countries. But even this is subject to various gradations. It may involve withdrawing the ambassador, but not officially closing the embassy. Sometimes, all diplomatic relations may be cut completely, as happened between the United States and Iran in 1980. In that case, Switzerland has represented US interests in Tehran and Pakistan has represented Iranian interests in the United

States. (The formal term for a country that represents another's interests in a third state is a "protecting power.")

Does a country need to have embassies and overseas missions?

Generally, states will want to engage with the international community to a greater or lesser degree. This means developing a network of embassies, consulates, and permanent representations to international organizations. However, the number of overseas missions a country has is highly variable. Major powers will have an extensive network of representation. For example, the United States has over 300 missions around the world and France and the United Kingdom have around 170 each. For many smaller countries, it is simply impossible to afford the costs of setting up many embassies. Some of the smaller Pacific island states therefore maintain just a handful. For instance, Kiribati currently has just two overseas missions—a high commission in Fiji and its permanent representation at the UN—as well as ten honorary consulates.

When choosing where to set up an embassy, states will pick the most significant states and institutions. At the top of the list is the UN. As it is the center of international multilateral diplomacy, every country has a permanent representative there. This allows contacts to be established between countries that do not have embassies in one another's capitals. After that, choices will usually be made based on significance and where special ties exist. The majority of countries have an embassy in Washington, DC. Similarly, many members of the Commonwealth and the Francophonie will retain missions in London and Paris respectively. (By a quirk of history, Commonwealth countries have high commissions in one other's capitals, rather than embassies. The functions are the same, though.) Meanwhile, the EU is also becoming an increasingly important location for an embassy. Although not a country, a mission to the EU allows countries to have a high degree of interaction with the twenty-seven members, all of which have large embassies in Brussels, as well as with key EU bodies dealing with joint foreign policy and trade.

Why is membership of the UN important?

Although recognition by other states is often an immediate priority, the single most important goal for any new state is to become a member of the UN. Founded in 1945 with 51 members, it is now made up of 193 states. The most recent member is South Sudan, which joined on July 14, 2011.

Membership of the UN is vital as it is widely understood to confirm that an entity is regarded as a state by the international community. Once a state joins the UN its independence and statehood is usually considered to be generally accepted and beyond serious doubt. Of course, this does not mean that every member of the UN is recognized by every other member. At present, six member states are not currently formally recognized by every other member: Israel (twenty-six members do not recognize it, including Saudi Arabia, Indonesia, Pakistan, Syria, and Iraq); the PRC (fourteen members, including Honduras, Nicaragua, and Haiti); North Korea (Japan and South Korea); South Korea (North Korea); Cyprus (Turkey); and Armenia (Pakistan). Nevertheless, UN membership marks the ultimate symbol of independence. Having said this, it is important to stress that the UN itself cannot recognize states. Formally speaking, there is no such thing as a "UN-recognized state." Only states can recognize states.

How does a country join the UN?

The process for joining the UN is laid down in Chapter II of the UN Charter. According to Article 4:

1. Membership in the United Nations is open to all other peace-loving states which accept the obligations

contained in the present Charter and, in the judgment of the Organization, are able and willing to carry out these obligations.

2. The admission of any such state to membership in the United Nations will be effected by a decision of the General Assembly upon the recommendation of the Security Council.

By convention, any state wishing to join must first submit a letter to the secretary-general asking to be admitted and stating that they abide by the principles of the organization. Following this, it must then receive a recommendation from the Security Council. Once the application is passed to the council, it will be sent to a committee for consideration. This will produce a report on the candidacy, noting whether the applicant meets the terms of statehood and whether it is able to meet the duties and responsibilities of UN membership. Once the report is received, and assuming it is positive, the application is put to the council. It then needs to gain positive votes from nine of the council's fifteen members. At the same time, it must not receive a negative vote from any of the five veto-wielding permanent members: the United Kingdom, China, France, Russia, and the United States. While the council will usually accept applications put to it by the secretary general, this is not always the case. For instance, in 2011 the United States rejected Palestine's application for membership. Once the Security Council has recommended membership, the candidate state must then receive two-thirds majority support in the General Assembly.

Overall, this can be a very quick process. For example, South Sudan became a member of the UN less than a week after declaring independence. Likewise, Montenegro, which became a member in June 2006, managed to join within weeks of its independence. Once full membership has been secured, a state can then join a range of bodies and organizations associated with the UN. These include the World Bank, the International Monetary Fund (IMF), the World Health Organization (WHO) and the UN Educational, Scientific, and Cultural Organization (UNESCO).

Could UN membership ever replace individual recognition?

Given the high degree of consensus needed to join the UN, and the disputes that have arisen over recognition in certain contentious cases, it has been suggested that the international community should perhaps move to a formal system of collective recognition based on UN membership. Indeed, it was even discussed during the drafting of the UN Charter, in 1945.[4] According to proponents of this, decisions would no longer be undertaken individually by states. Instead, they would be made according to the UN member admission process or perhaps reviewed by the International Court of Justice to remove the element of politics from the decision.

It is certainly an alluring idea. It would get rid of arbitrary or self-interested recognition decisions by individual states. However, while it would possibly add a degree of coherence to recognition, the idea has been roundly rejected by states. As they see it, such a process would be an unacceptable challenge to their sovereign prerogative to decide if or when to recognize another country. For this reason, it seems extremely unlikely that collective recognition by an international body, such as the UN, will replace individual recognition in the future.

What are the alternatives to full UN membership?

While full membership of the UN is clearly the primary aspiration for every state, this is not always possible. For

4. United Nations, *Documents of the United Nations Conference on International Organization, San Francisco, 1945*, Volume VII (London and New York: United Nations, 1945–1946), p. 30.

example, as noted, Palestine's membership, while supported by most of the world, is opposed by the United States. Likewise, Kosovo's membership would be blocked by Russia and China's veto.

In such circumstances, there are several alternative options. The first of these is to obtain the status of nonmember state or permanent observer, (more precisely defined as, a "Nonmember State having received a standing invitation to participate as observers in the sessions and the work of the General Assembly and maintaining permanent observer missions at Headquarters"). Unlike full membership, this does not require Security Council approval. Instead, it is based solely on a vote of the General Assembly. In a previous era, this was often seen as first step toward full membership. Indeed, practically every state that has held this status in the past has gone on to become a full member, including Austria, Finland, Italy, and Japan. At present, there are just two observer states: the Vatican and Palestine. Some have suggested that Kosovo should also pursue this route. However, fearful that it would become stuck with this status, Pristina would prefer to wait and see if the situation will change and it can achieve full membership.

Another option, which can be run in parallel with being a non-member state, is to seek membership of specific UN bodies. This can provide a way to gain increasing international acceptance as a state, pending full admission to the UN. This has been done in several instances. For example, in June 2009, Kosovo was admitted to the World Bank and the IMF. This was possible because the two organizations have a weighted voting system that favors economically strong countries such as the United States, Japan, Germany, the United Kingdom, and France; all of which supported Kosovo's independence. More recently, in October 2011, Palestine became a member of UNESCO on a simple majority vote (107 votes in favor, 4 against, and 52 abstentions). Meanwhile, the Pacific island states of

Niue and the Cook Islands, both of which are in free association with New Zealand, while not members of the UN are members of several UN bodies and institutions, such as WHO and UNESCO.

What other international organizations can states join?

Although UN membership is the primary goal for any new state, there are a host of other bodies that a new state can join. These fall into several categories and vary dramatically in size. First, there are the regional organizations. These include the Organization of American States (OAS), the Caribbean Community (CARICOM), the EU, the Commonwealth of Independent States (CIS), the AU, the Arab League, the Gulf Cooperation Council (GCC), the Association of Southeast Asian States (ASEAN), the Pacific Islands Forum, and the Economic Community of West African States (ECOWAS). The smallest of these, the GCC has just six members. The largest, the African Union, has fifty-five. In some instances, membership is a straightforward procedure and is automatically open to any new regional state. For others, such as the EU, it is a lengthy and complicated procedure. A state needs to go through an extensive accession process that requires significant adaptation to the laws and principles of the body. This can take well over a decade.

As well as regional bodies, there are a multitude of other organizations that new states can join. Some represent loose collections of states that share a broadly similar political commitment. For example, the Non-Aligned Movement, which has 120 members, represents states that are not tied to a major geopolitical bloc, such as NATO, which provides collective defense for its 30 members from Europe and North America, or the far looser Shanghai Cooperation Organization, which brings together Russia, China, and four Central Asian states. Other organizations are designed to provide a platform for dialogue on important issues. For example, the International

Organization for Migration (IOM) provides advice on "humane and orderly migration" for its 157 members and 10 observer states. The Council of Europe promotes human rights, the development of democratic values, and the preservation of cultural heritage among its forty-six member states. The Organization for Security and Cooperation in Europe (OSCE) is a forum for discussion on crisis and conflict management for fifty-seven countries across Europe, Central Asia, and North America.

Then there are bodies designed to facilitate economic interaction and development. One of the most important of these is the World Trade Organization, which deals with the rules of trade between states. Other key development institutions are known as international financial institutions (IFIs). As well as the World Bank and the IMF, these include the European Bank for Reconstruction and Development (EBRD), the Asian Development Bank, the African Development Bank, and the Inter-American Development Bank.

Additionally, some organizations represent clubs for groups of states that share historic or cultural ties. For example, the Organization of Islamic Cooperation (OIC) brings together fifty-seven predominantly Muslim states. The Commonwealth of Nations (fifty-three members) and the Francophonie (fifty-four members) provide a forum for discussion for countries that were, respectively, part of the British Empire or where French is the mother tongue or is widely spoken. Interestingly, in recent years both the Commonwealth and Francophonie have attracted new members that do not fit these traditional descriptions. For example, Mozambique, a former Portuguese colony, joined the Commonwealth in 1995 and Rwanda, a former Belgian and German colony, joined in 2009. Meanwhile, countries as diverse as Thailand (2008), the United Arab Emirates (2010), Montenegro (2010), Mexico (2014), and Kosovo (2014) have all become part of the French-speaking world.

What other steps are needed to join the international community?

Gaining recognition and joining leading regional and international organizations are obviously important steps toward widespread acceptance. However, there are many other things that a new country needs to do to become a fully integrated member of the international community. These include completing the practical measures that link countries to one another. For instance, joining the International Telecommunications Union (ITU) is vital for obtaining a telephone dialing code and joining the Universal Postal Union (UPU) ensures that a country is recognized as part of the global mail system. A new state also must obtain two- and three-letter country codes, which are issued by the International Organization for Standardization (ISO). An internet top-level domain name is also an important goal for new states.

As well as the main political and economic international organizations, there are a host of other intergovernmental institutions that new states will want to join. For example, joining the International Criminal Police Organization (INTERPOL) and World Customs Organization (WCO) means that a state's police forces and customs authorities can cooperate more easily with their counterparts abroad. Meanwhile, the Permanent Court of Arbitration provides an important mechanism for dispute resolution. Likewise, new states will often want to encourage various national bodies to join their relevant international associations. These bodies could include chambers of commerce, humanitarian organizations, and professional associations.

Additionally, a state's presence on the world stage can be enhanced in several other ways. Participating in major sporting and cultural events is a particularly significant way of announcing that a state has arrived. New states will therefore often attach significance to organizations like the International Olympic Committee (IOC) and FIFA, the governing body for world soccer. (Although both organizations are, under certain circumstances, also open to territories that are not independent.) In fact, in many ways, taking part in the Olympic Games and the FIFA World Cup are more emblematic of statehood for many ordinary people than participation in formal political or economic bodies. As one diplomat said at the time of Kosovo's declaration of independence, Serbia would not accept that Kosovo is a state until it sees it playing in the soccer World Cup. While this has not happened yet, Kosovo sent athletes to the Rio and Tokyo Olympic Games in 2016 and 2021, respectively. At a cultural level, events like the annual Eurovision Song Contest also attract huge audiences—183 million in May 2021—and participation in them can therefore become important goals for new states.

In cases where statehood is uncontroversial, many of these steps are mere formalities and can often be completed relatively quickly. In cases of contested statehood, the picture is often shaped by the degree of political support a claimant enjoys. Sometimes, membership of an organization is entirely up to the organization itself. Others, to avoid controversy, have opted to use UN membership as a criterion. At one stage, the national soccer authority of a state that is not a member of the UN couldn't join UEFA, the governing body for soccer in Europe. However, there is rarely any obvious logic to this as some UN organizations do not require UN membership. For instance, although both the ITU and the UPU are formally part of the UN system, membership is open to any state that can get the support of two thirds of the members.

How can countries prevent breakaway regions from being recognized?

While joining international bodies is usually uncontroversial for states that have broken away with permission, it is far more problematic in cases of unilateral secession. States facing an act of unilateral secession will often wage an intense diplomatic battle to stop, or at least limit, recognition. There are several elements to such a counter-secession strategy. First, the country trying to prevent recognition must make sure that everyone understands that it strongly opposes the attempt to break away. Outside states will often base their decision on whether to recognize a new state on the way that the parent state behaves. If it looks as though it will eventually accept the new state, then they will take this as their cue to interact with the seceding territory, if not recognize it. A state can signal its opposition in several ways. For instance, it can issue a statement clarifying its position or annul the declaration of independence. Often, a state will also want to signal its ongoing claim to sovereignty by maintaining nominal institutions, such as local councils, and electing parliamentarians from these areas. Obviously, they may not have a physical presence in the territory, or effective control, but it is important to keep up appearances for domestic and international purposes.

The second element is to focus on preventing the state from being recognized by other states and admitted to international organizations. Ideally, the most powerful weapon is some form of decision on collective non-recognition. In this regard, a UN resolution condemning the act of secession is the ideal goal. Failing this, then a lot will depend on the allies a state has. Great powers are very important, though not necessarily decisive, in determining whether an attempted secession ultimately succeeds or fails. Additionally, it is important to prevent the breakaway territory from being admitted into UN bodies or other organizations. But even if a state is successful in stopping a seceding territory from being recognized or admitted into major political and economic organizations, it also must ensure that the territory is prevented from gaining any sort of legitimization that may eventually pave the way for widespread acceptance and recognition, for example by participating in sporting and cultural events.

Finally, there is the option of legal action. This can be done in a variety of ways. One obvious route is to bring a case before the International Court of Justice, as Serbia did with Kosovo. However, other options can be pursued, including by private individuals. For example, the fact that Northern Cyprus remains a sovereign part of the Republic of Cyprus, and that the TRNC is merely a subordinate regime to Turkey, was confirmed by the European Court of Human Rights in a case brought by a refugee who had been unable to return to her property.[5] While pursuing the legal route to confirm sovereignty may seem to be an obvious option, many states are nevertheless wary of doing so. There is always the risk that the court may in fact return an unfavorable result.

What is "Taiwanization"?

"Taiwanization" refers to the process whereby a de facto state is widely accepted and interacts openly with other states and organizations but is not recognized by them as a sovereign independent state. The term comes from the way in which Taiwan, while no longer enjoying widespread recognition, has nevertheless retained considerable international ties. As well as maintaining regularized relations with many governments, it also participates in many international organizations and takes part in sporting and cultural activities, including the Olympic Games (as "Chinese Taipei"). In truth, the term is a misnomer as Taiwan is not technically a case of contested statehood but a case of competing claims to government.

Regardless of the accuracy of the term, Taiwanization has long been the most realistic foreign policy goal for de facto states, at least in the short to medium term. With little hope for them of gaining formal recognition, it offers a chance to break out of the isolation that most self-declared states endure. It also provides the hope that with the passage of time,

---

5. European Court of Human Rights, Loizidou v. Turkey (no. 15318/89), Judgment (Merits), November 28, 1996.

and greater normalization, recognition may eventually follow. Many parent states therefore see Taiwanization as a very real threat. For example, while the Cypriot government believes the TRNC has little hope of gaining widespread recognition for the foreseeable future, it is very acutely aware that it could gain widespread acceptance and fears that this will reduce Turkish Cypriot desire for reunification. Preventing the Taiwanization of Northern Cyprus has therefore tended to be Nicosia's most important goal in its counter-secession efforts. More recently, Kosovo has increasingly come to be seen by many de facto states as a better model to follow—even if the term "Kosovoization," which has been used, is rather unwieldy.

Can states interact without recognizing each other?

Certainly. Where the two countries concerned are both members of the UN, the question of interaction is usually more likely to be about managing domestic and international political sensitivities, rather than any specific worry about legalizing the existence of the other territory. After all, they will regularly sit in the hall of the General Assembly together. For instance, Israel maintains contacts, even fairly extensive ones, with some of the twenty-six UN members that do not formally recognize it.

In cases involving a UN member and a territory that is not a member of the UN, the situation can be rather more complicated. The extent of interaction—often termed "engagement without recognition"—will depend on a variety of factors. In some cases, a state will want to minimize its contact with a de facto state as much as possible, if not avoid any sort of interaction altogether, to show that it does not accept it as an independent entity and will not legitimize its existence. At other times, some form of interaction, even if very limited, must occur. For one thing, states' responsibility to ensure the basic well-being of their citizens abroad applies to unrecognized states no less than recognized ones. In addition, it may be necessary to help encourage a de facto state to take part in a peace process with the parent state. At other times, a state may be perfectly happy to have extensive interaction with a de facto state that it cannot formally recognize for domestic political reasons or because it does not want to antagonize an international partner.

Perhaps the most important thing to bear in mind is that intent is vital when it comes to recognition. For recognition to have occurred there must be some clear indication that this was the explicit wish of a state. There is no such thing as accidental recognition. However, even if a state continues to insist that it does not recognize the other state, there is a lot of room for cooperation. As a result, there is a high degree of latitude concerning engagement without recognition. Indeed, such engagement can seem radical. Perhaps the best example came in March 2013 when the foreign minister of Kosovo was welcomed at the Greek foreign ministry in Athens and was even officially described as the foreign minister of Kosovo at a press conference. However, because the Greek foreign minister stressed that this did not mark a change of his country's policy of non-recognition, this was not deemed to amount to recognition; even though this could be construed by any reasonable measure to have amounted to recognition in all but name. Of course, the requirement of intent does not provide a state with a completely free hand. There are certain steps that cannot be taken. For example, opening an embassy or signing a bilateral treaty establishing formal diplomatic relations would necessarily amount to recognition. Nevertheless, there is considerable room for a state to interact with a de facto state if it so wishes.

7

CURRENT QUESTIONS AND FUTURE DIRECTIONS

Can states cease to exist?

Yes, although it is becoming increasingly unusual. While estimates vary considerably, it is thought that around 200 states have ceased to exist since the start of the nineteenth century. That means on average one state has disappeared a year. However, of this number, only ten or so have disappeared since 1945. This would seem to suggest that "state death" or "state extinction," as the phenomenon is more generally known, is now rather rare in international politics.

Broadly speaking, there are three distinct ways that a state may cease to exist: conquest, dissolution, and merger. Traditionally, conquest has been the most common form of state extinction. Over the course of history, numerous countries have been invaded and annexed by another state and thus disappeared. However, military conquest is now exceedingly rare. Today, it is accepted that acts of conquest will not be recognized, even after many decades have elapsed. The best example was when the Baltic republics—Estonia, Latvia, and Lithuania—broke away from the Soviet Union in 1991 and their sovereignty was reaffirmed by the United States and others. Of course, we still see occasional cases where part of a state may be invaded and occupied, such as Russia's annexation of Crimea in 2014. However, such acts leading to the extinction of a sovereign state are now extremely unusual—in fact Iraq's forcible annexation of Kuwait in 1990 is the only example in recent decades—and highly unlikely to be recognized by the wider international community. The second way in which states can cease to exist is by dissolution. Obvious examples of this are the extinction of the Soviet Union, Czechoslovakia, and Yugoslavia. Third, there are mergers. There have been instances where a state has given up its independence to unite with another state. In the post-1945 era, examples include the short-lived United Arab Republic (between Egypt and Syria, 1958–1961), Tanzania (1964), the Republic of Vietnam (1975), the German Democratic Republic (1990), and the Republic of Yemen (1990).

Of course, the specific circumstances varied. For example, as we saw earlier, in the case of North and South Yemen, it was understood that the two previous sovereign entities ceased to exist, and an entirely new state came into being. However, since both North and South Yemen had been members of the UN, the new state did not have to go through an admissions procedure. In contrast, the unification of Germany saw the five states of East Germany—the German Democratic Republic— accede to the Federal Republic of Germany. East Germany ceased to exist.

Could climate change lead to state extinction?

In addition to the forms of state death described in the last section, there is in fact another possible way in which a state could conceivably cease to exist—albeit one that has never been seen before. As noted at the start of the book, international law is clear that one of the key characteristics of statehood is a defined territory. If a state physically loses its land, it is no longer a state. Until now, the prospect of a country losing its statehood in this manner has been purely hypothetical. It has never happened in the real world. However, global warming and climate change have made this a very real prospect. There are now at least four states in the Pacific and Indian oceans—Kiribati, Maldives, the Marshall Islands, and Tuvalu—that are facing the very real prospect that they may be submerged under rising sea levels. Although they are actively investigating ways to preserve their sovereignty, the international community may eventually have to accept that these states no longer exist as formal sovereign entities and that they have no realistic prospect of revival. What would happen then is unclear. It would be a wholly unprecedented development in international affairs.

Of course, if any states were to disappear due to climate change, then some serious thought would have to be given to the question of de-recognition. At present, there is no mechanism for addressing this situation and, so far, policymakers have never even seriously considered this situation. However, it is not as simple as merely saying that the country in question has ceased to exist and is therefore no longer recognized. There may well be bilateral issues to manage, including the ownership of diplomatic property or the fate of citizens of that state living in another country. Another factor to consider would be the state's membership of the UN and other international bodies. This could also create a range of serious legal and political problems.

Can we now think of two classes of states—de facto states and "real" ones?

One of the more interesting aspects of the rise of secessionist territories that have proclaimed independence, but have yet to receive recognition, is that we appear to be moving into a strange new era in which there are a growing number of states that are recognized by some countries but not by others. Not so very long ago, such a situation seemed absurd. No longer. Within the international system, we can even grade states according to the degree of recognition they have received.

At the top of the hierarchy are those states that are UN members and enjoy full recognition by all other members. Then there are a small number of states that are members of the UN but are not recognized by all the other members. These include Israel, the PRC, North Korea, South Korea, Cyprus, and Armenia. Next are those states that have not joined the UN but have received a high degree of recognition and have managed to join several international organizations and institutions. This category would include Kosovo, Palestine, Taiwan, and Western Sahara. After these are the states that managed to be recognized by at least one UN member, but have very little wider acceptance, such as the TRNC, Abkhazia, and South Ossetia. (The entities of Donetsk and Luhansk, in Ukraine, have been recognized by Russia but by general agreement do not meet even the basic criteria of statehood.) Following them are the territories that essentially meet the criteria of statehood, aspire to recognition, but have not been admitted to the UN or recognized by any UN member states, such as Somaliland, Iraqi Kurdistan, Transnistria, and Nagorno-Karabakh. Of course, some, such as Somaliland and Kurdistan, have a great deal of international sympathy and have widespread engagement. In contrast, Nagorno-Karabakh and Transnistria have minimal international interaction.

All this has given rise to a range of anomalies as well as many odd relationships. Some territories with limited recognition recognize each other. For example, the breakaway states in the former Soviet Union—South Ossetia, Abkhazia, Nagorno-Karabakh, and Transnistria—have all recognized each other. However, none of them have recognized the TRNC. Meanwhile, the TRNC will not recognize Kosovo because it knows that it will not be recognized in return. Although Turkey was one of the main proponents of Kosovo's independence, and Pristina maintains good relations with Ankara, Kosovo does not want to upset its supporters within the EU. Likewise, although Taiwan recognized Kosovo within days of its declaration of independence, Kosovo will not recognize Taiwan in return for fear of antagonizing China, whose vote it will need if it ever wants to join the UN. Meanwhile, Palestine refuses to recognize Kosovo, regarding its declaration of statehood as an illegal act of secession. Finally, Russia recognizes Abkhazia and South Ossetia but does not recognize Transnistria. But Transnistria does appear to be recognized by Abkhazia and South Ossetia.

Is it time to reconsider opposition to unilateral secession?

While the pace of state creation may have slowed, it has not ended. Sub-state groups continue to demand independence in every region of the globe, in rich as well as poor countries, in democracies as well as dictatorships, in ancient as well as recently established states. They do so despite the international community's general preference for the territorial integrity of their parent states.

This begs the question as to whether the international community should continue to deny territories the right of unilateral secession. Kosovo has demonstrated that it is difficult to oppose in every single case, as did Bangladesh in the early 1970s. There are instances when unilateral secession should be legitimate. But the Balkan case also revealed the critical importance of a principled, as opposed to unilateral or ad hoc, approach to unilateral secession and other types of state creation. Acts that could have global effects, especially if those effects could lead to violence, need to be publicly justifiable according to clearly spelled out and generally applicable norms. In a state system without an overarching authority, and without firmly settled ways to interpret changes to long-standing practices, there is a danger that any unilateral change will be used by other states, especially great powers, to justify their own decisions to break with these established practices. This was seen most clearly when Russia cited the Kosovo "precedent" to justify its recognition of the unilateral secessions of Abkhazia, South Ossetia, Crimea, and Donetsk and Luhansk. Such cycles undermine international law and order.

Perhaps the time is ripe to rethink the entire approach to unilateral secession. One approach might be to revisit the principles of de facto statehood that guided the international community in the era before decolonization. This sought to balance a liberal conception of the legitimate interests and rights of the secessionists, parent states, and third states. It was based on two core principles, which are still, from time to time, proclaimed but are not necessarily practiced. First, nonintervention by coercive means into the rival claims of statehood between the secessionists and the parent states. Second, the recognition of new states—with or without consent of their parent states— only if these entities are independent of external authorities and maintain a government that has effective control over the claimed territory and population.

There is nothing simple about responding to violent secessionist conflicts, yet there are both practical and normative problems with the current practice of affirming the territorial integrity of parent states in the face of secessionist claims. The practical problem is that it is very difficult to mediate secessionist conflicts if outsiders insist on the continuing unity of the parent state as the starting point. Unless one party to the dispute is very weak, mediation is likely going to be successful only when mediators are neutral and impartial with respect to the core issue of contention. Why should Georgia, Azerbaijan, or Moldova compromise on the status of their secessionist territories when their territorial integrity is internationally guaranteed to begin with? If the breakaway territories can resist parent state control on the ground, then the external affirmation of territorial integrity of those parent states is a recipe for never-ending conflict and possible involvement of outside countries, as happened in these three cases. It also leads to de facto states that are unanswerable internationally for their actions.

There is also an important normative problem. As numerous leading foreign policymakers—including John Quincy Adams, Lord Castlereagh, George Canning, Abraham Lincoln, and Woodrow Wilson—argued, it should not be the business of international society to affirm or guard the territorial integrity of states against internal challenges from their own citizens. That perpetuates states regardless of the treatment or wishes of their population. In their view, it was up to each country to earn the loyalty and allegiance of its inhabitants. Once the links of loyalty were broken, the normative case for de facto statehood as the standard for recognition rested on the presumed will of the population in question to form the new state. As suggested in Chapter 2, since there was typically no agreement between the secessionists and the parent states on who is entitled to independence and/or by what procedure can that entitlement be exercised, the formation of a stable, effective entity in which the population habitually obeyed the new rulers was taken as an authoritative expression of the collective will of the people to constitute an independent state. The lack of agreement between secessionists and parent states on the right of secessionists to statehood and/or by what procedure that right can be exercised is still the defining feature of nearly all contemporary secessionist situations.

There is an additional reason why effective statehood as the standard of recognition should be considered: effective statehood is the opposite of failed or quasi statehood, which is detrimental not only to the citizens of a territory, but also to third countries. If recognized states cannot effectively control the population and territory they claim—as was the case for the Congo, Angola, Mozambique, Georgia, Croatia, Bosnia and Herzegovina, Azerbaijan, Moldova, or FRY at the time of their recognition—one of two things have tended to happen. Either there has been lasting internal conflict, which besides bringing misery to the local population can have external spillover effects, or outsiders have chosen forcible intervention to prevent their territorial disintegration, as in the Congo, Bosnia and Herzegovina, and the FRY. As seen, these interventions have often brought challenges as they require costly and intrusive involvement on the ground, with no promise of an internally legitimate, self-sustaining state once the international presence ends. They also revealed real limits to the willingness of states to shoulder responsibility for other societies. The controversial decision by many countries to permit Kosovo's unilateral declaration of independence was at least partially motivated by the desire to cease bearing the burden of what promised to be an endless and adversarial governance of a restive majority demanding independence and willing to resist at all costs a return to Serbian rule.

If there is persistent conflict over statehood, there would seem to be a case to be made that outside parties should try to minimize any harmful effects of the contest and explore any possible compromise solution. Crucially, this should not exclude independence and even border changes. If the international system is to remain a system of self-governed independent states, then as difficult as it may be to accomplish, it could be argued that the primary international response to destabilizing developments within existing states should be the creation of functioning states that control their territory and enjoy—or can be reasonably presumed to enjoy—the allegiance of their population. If a new state is to be recognized, it can be asked, as a prerequisite to recognition, to fulfil various conditions, including meeting certain thresholds of human and minority rights, as a way of resolving any disputes accompanying its birth.

Will we ever see a world without "states"?

The idea of states is now so entrenched in international thinking that it becomes hard to think of a world in which the basic unit of political organization is anything other than the state, or something very similar. And yet, we do seem to be seeing a certain shift away from the traditional conceptions of statehood.

Perhaps the best example of this is the EU. Made up of states, it cannot be described as an international organization.

It is much more than that. Yet it is quite clearly not a state, or even a "superstate." (Some have said that it is best described as a "political community.") The members retain their own legal identities and sovereignty, but the EU also has a legal personality and can enter treaties with other countries and organizations. It negotiates with a single voice on trade issues, but in other areas of foreign policy, members remain free to make their individual decisions—but may act collectively if they so wish.

The EU in many ways represents an interesting example of how small and medium-sized states have seen the benefits of a degree of pooled sovereignty in certain areas, while retaining their individual political structures. The idea is catching on elsewhere. We are seeing other groups of states pooling elements of their sovereignty in the same sort of ways as the EU. For example, shared structures are emerging in the Caribbean, from a shared currency and joint defense through to single judicial institutions. The key question is whether these regional groupings retain their current hybrid systems or whether, with the passage of time, they too evolve into states. However, none of these developments move in a foreordained direction. As the decision of the United Kingdom to leave the EU—Brexit—has shown, the popular urges for states to remain autonomous actors on the international stage are still strong and may prevail.

Does statehood still matter?

There is no doubt that we live in a world where many of the old certainties can change rapidly. The ever evolving international environment is calling into question many of the long-held assumptions about the nature of the international system and international relations. There is no doubt that we live in a world where states are no longer the only major international actor. International organizations and major corporations play an increasingly important role in the international system. And yet, states remain very much at the heart of that system.

They are still the fundamental reference point for most of us. They are still the primary subjects of international law. The UN is still a body composed of states. Countries still talk primarily to countries. For all these reasons, states and statehood still matter. And for as long as states still matter, there will be people chasing the dream of establishing their own sovereign independent countries within the wider international community of states.

Appendix A

GROWTH OF UN

MEMBERSHIP, 1945–

1945 (51) Argentina, Australia, Belgium, Bolivia, Brazil,
            Byelorussian Soviet Socialist Republic (Belarus
            1991), Canada, Chile, China, Colombia,
            Costa Rica, Cuba, Czechoslovakia, Denmark,
            Dominican Republic, Ecuador, Egypt, El
            Salvador, Ethiopia, France, Greece, Guatemala,
            Haiti, Honduras, India, Iran, Iraq, Lebanon,
            Liberia, Luxembourg, Mexico, Netherlands, New
            Zealand, Nicaragua, Norway, Panama, Paraguay,
            Peru, Philippine Republic (Philippines 1947),
            Poland, Saudi Arabia, Syria, Turkey, Ukrainian
            Soviet Socialist Republic (Ukraine 1991), Union
            of South Africa (South Africa 1961), Union of
            Soviet Socialist Republics (Russian Federation
            1991), United Kingdom, United States, Uruguay,
            Venezuela, Yugoslavia

1946 (55) Afghanistan, Iceland, Siam (Thailand
            1949), Sweden

1947 (57) Pakistan, Yemen

1948 (58)	Burma (Myanmar 1989)
1949 (59)	Israel
1950 (60)	Indonesia
1955 (76)	Albania, Austria, Bulgaria, Cambodia, Ceylon (Sri Lanka 1991), Finland, Hungary, Ireland, Italy, Jordan, Laos, Libya, Nepal, Portugal, Romania, Spain
1956 (80)	Japan, Morocco, Sudan, Tunisia
1957 (82)	Ghana, Federation of Malaya (Malaysia 1963)
1958 (82¹)	Guinea
1960 (99)	Cameroun, Central African Republic, Chad, Congo (Brazzaville) (Congo 1971), Congo (Leopoldville) (Democratic Republic of Congo 1997), Cyprus, Dahomey (Benin 1974), Gabon, Ivory Coast, Malagasy Republic (Madagascar 1975), Mali, Niger, Nigeria, Senegal, Somalia, Togo, Upper Volta (Burkina Faso 1984)
1961 (104²)	Mauritania, Mongolia, Sierra Leone, Tanganyika (Tanzania 1964)
1962 (110)	Algeria, Burundi, Jamaica, Rwanda, Trinidad and Tobago, Uganda
1963 (113)	Kenya, Kuwait, Zanzibar
1964 (115³)	Malawi, Malta, Zambia
1965 (118)	Gambia, Maldive Islands, Singapore
1966 (122)	Barbados, Botswana, Guyana, Lesotho
1967 (123)	Democratic Yemen
1968 (126)	Equatorial Guinea, Mauritius, Swaziland
1970 (127)	Fiji
1971 (132)	Bahrain, Bhutan, Oman, Qatar, United Arab Emirates

1. Egypt and Syria merged to form the United Arab Republic (UAR).
2. Syria left the United Arab Republic and retook its seat.
3. Zanzibar united with Tanganyika to form Tanzania.

1973 (135)	Bahamas, Federal Republic of Germany, German Democratic Republic
1974 (138)	Bangladesh, Grenada, Guinea-Bissau
1975 (144)	Cape Verde, Comoros, Mozambique, Papua New Guinea, Sao Tome and Principe, Suriname
1976 (147)	Angola, Samoa, Seychelles
1977 (149)	Djibouti, Viet Nam
1978 (151)	Dominica, Solomon Islands
1979 (152)	Saint Lucia
1980 (154)	Saint Vincent and the Grenadines, Zimbabwe
1981 (157)	Antigua and Barbuda, Belize, Vanuatu
1983 (158)	Saint Christopher and Nevis (Saint Kitts and Nevis 1986)
1984 (159)	Brunei Darussalam
1990 (159[4])	Liechtenstein, Namibia
1991 (166)	Democratic People's Republic of Korea, Estonia, Latvia, Lithuania, Marshall Islands, Federated States of Micronesia, Republic of Korea
1992 (179)	Armenia, Azerbaijan, Bosnia and Herzegovina, Croatia, Georgia, Kazakhstan, Kyrgyzstan, Republic of Moldova, San Marino, Slovenia, Tajikistan, Turkmenistan, Uzbekistan
1993 (184[5])	Andorra, Czech Republic, Eritrea, Monaco, Slovakia, The former Yugoslav Republic of Macedonia
1994 (185)	Palau
1999 (188)	Kiribati, Nauru, Tonga
2000 (189[6])	Federal Republic of Yugoslavia, Tuvalu

4. German Democratic Republic merged with Federal Republic of Germany and Yemen and merged with Democratic Yemen.
5. Czechoslovakia ceased to exist and was replaced by the Czech Republic and Slovakia.
6. The Socialist Federal Republic of Yugoslavia ceased to exist in 1992. The Federal Republic of Yugoslavia was admitted as a new member in 2000.

2002 (191)   Switzerland, Timor-Leste
2006 (192)   Montenegro
2011 (193)   South Sudan

Source: Growth in United Nations membership, United Nations. https://www.un.org/en/about-us/growth-in-un-membership

Appendix B

UN GENERAL ASSEMBLY
RESOLUTION 1514 (XV), 1960

Declaration on the Granting of Independence to Colonial Countries and Peoples

Adopted by General Assembly resolution 1514 (XV) of 14 December 1960

The General Assembly,

Mindful of the determination proclaimed by the peoples of the world in the Charter of the United Nations to reaffirm faith in fundamental human rights, in the dignity and worth of the human person, in the equal rights of men and women and of nations large and small and to promote social progress and better standards of life in larger freedom,

Conscious of the need for the creation of conditions of stability and well-being and peaceful and friendly relations based on respect for the principles of equal rights and self-determination of all peoples, and of universal respect for, and observance of, human rights and fundamental freedoms for all without distinction as to race, sex, language or religion,

Recognizing the passionate yearning for freedom in all dependent peoples and the decisive role of such peoples in the attainment of their independence,

Aware of the increasing conflicts resulting from the denial of or impediments in the way of the freedom of such peoples, which constitute a serious threat to world peace,

Considering the important role of the United Nations in assisting the movement for independence in Trust and Non-Self-Governing Territories,

Recognizing that the peoples of the world ardently desire the end of colonialism in all its manifestations,

Convinced that the continued existence of colonialism prevents the development of international economic cooperation, impedes the social, cultural and economic development of dependent peoples and militates against the United Nations ideal of universal peace,

Affirming that peoples may, for their own ends, freely dispose of their natural wealth and resources without prejudice to any obligations arising out of international economic cooperation, based upon the principle of mutual benefit, and international law,

Believing that the process of liberation is irresistible and irreversible and that, in order to avoid serious crises, an end must be put to colonialism and all practices of segregation and discrimination associated therewith,

Welcoming the emergence in recent years of a large number of dependent territories into freedom and independence, and recognizing the increasingly powerful trends towards freedom in such territories which have not yet attained independence,

Convinced that all peoples have an inalienable right to complete freedom, the exercise of their sovereignty and the integrity of their national territory,

Solemnly proclaims the necessity of bringing to a speedy and unconditional end colonialism in all its forms and manifestations;

And to this end declares that:

1. The subjection of peoples to alien subjugation, domination and exploitation constitutes a denial of fundamental human rights, is contrary to the Charter of the United Nations and is an impediment to the promotion of world peace and co-operation.

2. All peoples have the right to self-determination; by virtue of that right they freely determine their political status and freely pursue their economic, social and cultural development.

3. Inadequacy of political, economic, social or educational preparedness should never serve as a pretext for delaying independence.

4. All armed action or repressive measures of all kinds directed against dependent peoples shall cease in order to enable them to exercise peacefully and freely their right to complete independence, and the integrity of their national territory shall be respected.

5. Immediate steps shall be taken, in Trust and Non-Self-Governing Territories or all other territories which have not yet attained independence, to transfer all powers to the peoples of those territories, without any conditions or reservations, in accordance with their freely expressed will and desire, without any distinction as to race, creed or color, in order to enable them to enjoy complete independence and freedom.

6. Any attempt aimed at the partial or total disruption of the national unity and the territorial integrity of a country is incompatible with the purposes and principles of the Charter of the United Nations.

7. All States shall observe faithfully and strictly the provisions of the Charter of the United Nations, the Universal Declaration of Human Rights and the present Declaration on the basis of equality, non-interference in the internal affairs of all States, and respect for the sovereign rights of all peoples and their territorial integrity.

RECOMMENDED READING

Armitage, David, *The Declaration of Independence: A Global History* (Cambridge, MA: Harvard University Press, 2007)

Bartkus, Viva O., *The Dynamics of Secession* (Cambridge: Cambridge University Press, 1999)

Brunet-Jailly, Emmanuel (editor), *Border Disputes: A Global Encyclopedia* [3 volumes] (Santa Barbara, California: ABC-Clio, 2014)

Buchheit, Lee C., *Secession: The Legitimacy of Self-Determination* (New Haven, CT: Yale University Press, 1978)

Buchanan, Allen, *Justice, Legitimacy, and Self-Determination: Moral Foundations for International Law* (Oxford: Oxford University Press, 2004)

Bühler, Konrad G., *State Succession and Membership in International Organizations: Legal Theories versus Political Pragmatism* (Leiden: Brill, 2001)

Caplan, Richard, *Europe and the Recognition of New States in Yugoslavia* (Cambridge: Cambridge University Press, 2005)

Caspersen, Nina, *Unrecognized States: The Struggle for Sovereignty in the Modern International System* (Cambridge: Polity, 2012)

Caspersen, Nina, and Gareth Stansfield (editors), *Unrecognized States in the International System* (London: Routledge, 2010)

Cassese, Antonio, *Self-Determination of Peoples: A Legal Reappraisal* (Cambridge: Cambridge University Press, 1995)

Chen, T., *The International Law of Recognition* (New York: Praeger, 1951)

Cobban, Alfred, *The Nation-State and National Self-Determination*, Revised edition (London: Collins, 1969)

Coggins, Bridget, *Power Politics and State Formation in the Twentieth Century: The Dynamics of Recognition* (Cambridge: Cambridge University Press, 2014)

Crawford, James, *The Creation of States in International Law*, 2nd edition (Oxford: Oxford University Press, 2006)

Daase, C., et al. (editors), *Recognition in International Relations* (Basingstoke: Palgrave Macmillan, 2015)

Davies, Norman, *Vanished Kingdoms: The History of Half-Forgotten Europe* (London: Allen Lane, 2011)

De Vries, Lotje, et al. (editors), *Secessionism in African Politics: Aspiration, Grievance, Performance, Disenchantment* (Basingstoke: Palgrave Macmillan: 2019)

Doyle, Don. H. (editor), *Secession as an International Phenomenon: From America's Civil War to Contemporary Separatist Movements* (Athens, GA: University of Georgia Press, 2010)

Fabry, Mikulas, *Recognizing States: International Society and the Establishment of New States since 1776* (Oxford: Oxford University Press, 2010)

Fazal, Tanisha M., *State Death: The Politics and Geography of Conquest, Occupation, and Annexation* (Princeton: Princeton University Press, 2007)

Fisch, Jörg, *The Right of Self-Determination of Peoples: The Domestication of an Illusion* (Cambridge: Cambridge University Press, 2015)

French, Duncan (editor), *Statehood and Self-Determination: Reconciling Tradition and Modernity in International Law* (Cambridge: Cambridge University Press, 2013)

Grant, Thomas D., *The Recognition of States: Law and Practice in Debate and Evolution* (Westport: Praeger, 1999)

Geldenhuys, Deon, *Contested States in World Politics* (Basingstoke: Palgrave Macmillan, 2009)

Grant, Thomas D., *Admission to the United Nations* (Leiden: Nijhoff, 2009)

Griffiths, Ryan D., *Age of Secession: The International and Domestic Determinants of State Birth* (Cambridge: Cambridge University Press, 2016)

Griffiths, Ryan D., *Secession and the Sovereignty Game: Strategy and Tactics for Aspiring Nations* (Ithaca, NY: Cornell University Press, 2021).

Griffiths, Ryan D., and Diego Muro (editors), *Strategies of Secession and Counter-Secession* (London: Rowman and Littlefield, 2020)

Gurr, Ted Robert, *People versus States: Minorities at Risk in the New Century* (Washington, DC: US Institute for Peace, 2000)

Heraclides, Alexis, *The Self-determination of Minorities in International Politics* (London: Frank Cass, 1991)

Jackson, Robert H, *Quasi-States: Sovereignty, International Relations and the Third World* (Cambridge: Cambridge University Press, 1990)

Ker-Lindsay, James, *The Foreign Policy of Counter Secession: Preventing the Recognition of Contested States* (Oxford: Oxford University Press, 2012)

Knop, Karen, *Diversity and Self-Determination in International Law* (Cambridge: Cambridge University Press, 2002)

Kohen, Marcelo G. (editor), *Secession: International Law Perspectives* (Cambridge: Cambridge University Press, 2006)

Kreijen, Gerard, *State Failure, Sovereignty and Effectiveness: Legal Lessons from the Decolonization of Sub-Saharan Africa* (Leiden: Martinus Nijhoff, 2004)

Lalonde, Suzanne, *Determining Boundaries in a Conflicted World: The Role of Uti Possidetis* (Montreal: McGill-Queen's University Press, 2002)

Lauterpacht, Hersch, *Recognition in International Law* (Cambridge: Cambridge University Press, 1947)

Manela, Erez, *The Wilsonian Moment: Self-Determination and the International Origins of Anti-Colonial Nationalism* (New York: Oxford University Press, 2007)

Marshall, Tim, *Worth Dying For: The Power and Politics of Flags* (London: Elliott & Thompson, 2016)

Middleton, Nick, *An Atlas of Countries That Don't Exist: A Compendium of Fifty Unrecognized and Largely Unnoticed States* (Basingstoke: Macmillan, 2016)

Moore, Margaret (editor), *National Self-Determination and Secession* (Oxford: Oxford University Press, 1998)

Musgrave, Thomas D., *Self-Determination and National Minorities* (Oxford: Clarendon Press, 1997)

O'Brien, William V. (editor), *The New Nations in International Law and Diplomacy* (London: Stevens and Sons, 1965)

O'Mahoney, Joseph, *Denying the Spoils of War: The Politics of Invasion and Non-Recognition* (Edinburgh: Edinburgh University Press, 2018)

Pavković, Aleksandar, with Peter Radan, *Creating New States: Theory and Practice of Secession* (Aldershot: Ashgate, 2007)

Pavković, Aleksandar, and Peter Radan, *The Ashgate Companion to Secession* (London: Routledge, 2011)

Pegg, Scott, *International Society and the De Facto State*
(Aldershot: Ashgate, 1999)
Pomerance, Michla, *Self-Determination in Law and Practice: The New
Doctrine in the United Nations* (The Hague: Martinus Nijhoff, 1982)
Raič, David, *Statehood and the Law of Self-Determination* (The
Hague: Kluwer Law International, 2002)
Roberts, Ivor (editor), *Satow's Diplomatic Practice*, 7th edition
(Oxford: Oxford University Press, 2018)
Roeder, Philip G., *Where Nation-States Come From: Institutional Change
in the Age of Nationalism* (Princeton, NJ: Princeton University
Press, 2007)
Qvortrup, Matt, *Referendums and Ethnic Conflict*
(Philadelphia: University of Pennsylvania Press, 2014)
Şen, İlker Gökhan, *Sovereignty Referendums in International and
Constitutional Law* (London: Springer, 2015)
Sorens, Jason, *Secessionism: Identity, Interest and Strategy*
(Montreal: McGill-Queen's University Press, 2012)
Talmon, Stefan, *Recognition of Governments in International Law*
(Oxford: Oxford University Press, 2006)
Tomuschat, Christian (editor), *Modern Law of Self-Determination*
(Dordrecht, The Netherlands: Martinus Nijhoff, 1993)
Visoka, Gezim, et al. (editors), *Routledge Handbook of State Recognition*
(London: Routledge: 2019)
Wellman, Christopher Heath, *A Theory of Secession: The Case for Political
Self-Determination* (Cambridge: Cambridge University Press, 2005)

INDEX